A D[...] REVELATION

A TREASURE HUNT

THE KANDEL

SISTERS

ISBN-13: 979-8-9891126-1-6

Cover photos via Unsplash.com (Honey Yanibel Minaya Cruz) and Istockphoto.com (byjeng, francisblack). Used by permission.

Unless otherwise indicated, all Scripture quotations are from the Holy Bible, New International Version®, NIV®. Copyright © 1973, 1978, 1984, 2011 by Biblica, Inc.™ Used by permission of Zondervan. All rights reserved worldwide. www.zondervan.com The "NIV" and "New International Version" are trademarks registered in the United States Patent and Trademark Office by Biblica, Inc.™

Other Scripture quotations include The Authorized (King James) Version. Rights in the Authorized Version in the United Kingdom are vested in the Crown. Reproduced by permission of the Crown's patentee, Cambridge University Press.

INTRODUCTION

Have you ever been on a treasure hunt or an archeological dig? We sisters haven't but have dreamed of joining one. Even as kids, working in our acres long garden, the idea of digging for buried treasure was far more exciting than the drudgery of hoeing the tomato plants or corn.

We all still love the hunt at antique malls and secondhand stores. Hey, some valuable stuff has been found in those places, so we're always up for the search.

Maybe that means we've always been treasure hunters at heart.

But have we ever found treasure?

The answer is yes.

Where?

In the pages of the Bible. And you know what? The book of Revelation is no different.

We say the name Revelation, and even saying it might stir up feelings of fear. We get it. It may drum up visions of apocalyptic events and scary stuff on the horizon. And some of the events in our world make the horizon seem a whole lot closer.

But here's the thing we want to camp on: this book offers a blessing, and if we want in on that, we need to read it, hear it, take it to heart.

But if you've picked up this book, *Revelation: A Treasure Hunt,* you don't have to go it alone. You can join us as we sit around the table and discuss the facets of this gem.

Actually, it's going to be a pretty easy read. Now there is some digging involved and a little sweat, but the end result is a new vision of Jesus Christ as He is unveiled in these pages.

So, grab your Bible, your trowel and pick, okay maybe your paper and pen. Get your coffee, your tea, your iced latte, or whatever makes you comfortable, and let's sit down together to talk about it.

We're going to take it slow, a journey of ninety days, so we can stop and smell the fragrance of the text.

If you have a question, write it down. Some of the questions might get answered as we dig a little deeper.

Now, join us as we open the book of Revelation and go on a treasure hunt.

REVELATION

CHAPTER 1

DAY 1

It started out normal enough, and then the threat of a pandemic inched its way into our vocabulary and onto our evening news. There was speculation about shutdowns, school closings, masks, and sheltering in. Suddenly it became all too real. A global pandemic was upon us. The whole world was catapulted into anxiety and fear. The questions started to come, are we living in the end times? Are these the last days?

Today, we look back at COVID 19 and shudder. It was an awful, scary, dreadful time. We talk about the quarantine and no, we won't soon forget, because the Coronavirus was one for the history books. Being away from family and friends, locked down, locked in, shopping restrictions, toilet paper shortages of all things, working from home, or just not working, fear was a major player in the world of 2020 and beyond.

We missed family gatherings, church services, concerts, movies, anywhere there were people, there were big restrictions. Sheltering at home, quarantined, is not a fun way to live. We are social beings, meant for fellowship.

However, this was not a first experience with a quarantine for us sisters. Years ago, our mom was diagnosed with scarlet fever, pretty serious in those days. The doctor was at the house when we got off the school bus. Kris and I thought it would serve us to complain that our throats hurt. Neither of us remember that our throats actually did hurt, but we said they did.

Smooth move.

And since you didn't mess around with scarlet fever, our house got quarantined and Kris and I got quarantined, in our bedroom, in our beds, with NO TV! Our meals were served to us in the bedroom and that should have been a highlight. It wasn't. Mom was ill; Dad wasn't a cook. Do the math. I only remember one meal and it wasn't memorable because it was good. It was a plateful of dried lima beans. They were crunchy. I still shudder. Ugh! Those were long boring days. But there was something that broke up the mundane. The doctor came every day for three days to give us shots. SHOTS! Linda, Kathie, and our two brothers got to hang out with Dad, run around in the sunshine, skip school, play, and WATCH TV. I think they drew pictures of shots and shoved them under the door.

Fun times!

Today, the COVID restrictions are mostly lifted. It's wonderful that we can get out, meet people to go for a walk, go to church, gather with family, hang out with friends, attend concerts, movies, there are no rules for grocery shopping, toilet paper is abundant, and not a lima bean in sight. We can praise God for all of that.

But was the pandemic a small taste of things to come? Are there some events on the horizon that lead us to believe that the days of the last book of the Bible may be upon us?

I realize that at first glance this book may seem scary. Are we in the last days the Revelation talks about? Are we entering the apocalypse?

Before we dive into chapter one, let's address the meaning of the word apocalypse. In our culture, it has come to mean a terrible, horrific, earthshaking event, where the planet is literally shaking. We use the word for natural events like hurricanes or earthquakes. Sci-fi loves to throw the word around in disaster movies.

And yet, that is not the meaning of the word. Apocalypse comes from the Greek word apokalypsis and contrary to popular belief, it doesn't mean an earth-shattering global catastrophe. The word simply means an unveiling, the lifting of a veil.

Have you been to a wedding where there is that glorious moment when the groom lifts his bride's veil to gaze into her eyes? He looks into the face of his beloved. His eyes, when he looks into her eyes, are filled with the pure joy and expectation for their beautiful future together.

I think God wants us to look at the book of Revelation that way. When the veil is lifted in this book and we open its pages, we can look into our Beloved Savior's eyes and see our beautiful future with Him.

And so, we begin to lift the veil on the book of Revelation.

The title of the book is singular. It is a Revelation, not revelations. The book is not so much about what is being revealed, but rather WHO is being revealed: Jesus Christ. When Jesus came to the earth, He came cloaked in humanity, so much so, that many did not recognize Him. In this book, the cloak is lifted, and we have the privilege of seeing Him in His glory and majesty. He is Savior, Redeemer, Lion of Judah, Lamb of God, Alpha and Omega, Beginning and End, First and Last, and everything in between. He is King over all other kings. He is the Lord of Lords and today He is seated in the heavens to rule and reign.

So, it is a glorious book, and if we will let it, reading and studying the Revelation can wrap us up in peace and rest, not fear and anxiety. My dear friends, God is on the throne, a very appropriate reminder for our world today.

DAY 2

Who wrote this book of the Bible? Ah, a trick question. The author of the book of Revelation is God. In reality, He is the author of this book and every other book of the Bible, but He chose to use men to write it down, scribes to record His very words.

"The revelation from Jesus Christ, which God gave him to show his servants what must soon take place. He made it known by sending his angel to his servant John, who testifies to everything he saw—that is, the word of God and the testimony of Jesus Christ." Revelation 1:1-2

God gave the message to Jesus, who sent an angel to His servant John, who was sharing this with God's servants.

Don't you love that? The supply chain: God to Jesus, to an angel, to John, and then to us. There's not a single interruption to this supply chain.

This book was written for us, for those who are His servants.

So, who was this John? Most scholars believe it to be John the disciple. He was not only one of the twelve disciples; he was one of the inner three. Often Jesus took Peter, James, and John with him. John had this beautiful relationship with Jesus. He is often referred to as the youngest of the disciples. He's the one Jesus trusted to care for His mother, Mary, when He was on the cross. John's job, before the Lord called him, was a fisherman, a simple fisherman. John didn't have any important letters after his name or any impressive titles before his name. But Jesus chose him, a young, wet behind the ears guy, and John became a devoted follower. Then he became a preacher, a pastor, an apostle, an evangelist, a missionary, and a writer of the Gospel of John, as well as the epistles of 1st, 2nd, and 3rd John. He wore a lot of hats in his lifetime and God used him greatly.

And don't you love that God could use him when he was very young? His youth was no hindrance to God's plan.

But now as Revelation begins, John was elderly. He probably no longer had the spring in his step that he once had, or the strength of his youth. And yet God had a brand-new assignment for him. John was now given the glorious task of writing down this Revelation. God was going to reveal amazing future events and John got to view them and record them.

And don't you just love that? Have you noticed there is a lot to love in this book?

God is never done with us. No matter our age, our circumstances, our physical abilities, or lack thereof, God has a plan. We aren't too young to be called; we aren't too old to be used. Even when we can't leave our homes, or if it comes to it, our beds, God can always use us because we can always pray.

What we know about John was that he was always a faithful follower of the Lord. We might have expected after all his years of faithful service that he would spend his last days basking in the sun on a beautiful island as a grand reward for his faith. That is not what happened. Here we read that in the last days of his life, he was exiled for his faith to an island of hard, volcanic rock, Patmos, a penal colony. This place was small; most accounts say it was just a few square miles. He didn't get to shelter at home. He sheltered in exile. The island of Patmos wasn't a vacation spot; it was barren, forsaken, a place for the forgotten of the world.

But God never forgot him. He was with him. And right there in the exile, the barrenness, the hard labor, the separation, the Lord gave him the exquisite, the majestic, the glorious.

John saw Jesus, the future, and heaven.

God gave John a taste of the amazing. What glorious vision of Jesus will we see if we redeem the time and spend it with Him? What new vision of who He is might we experience?

We can know that just like God didn't abandon John, He never abandons us.

Rest in that.

DAY 3

What is blessing? Is it health? Wealth? Prosperity? Yes, all of those are wonderful blessings, and we should thank God for our health, our finances, the abundance we have, and much, much more. But those things are fleeting. They can be here today and gone tomorrow.

It was the week before Thanksgiving and time for the routine mammogram. Not fun, but necessary. We sisters think if we must do it, we might as well do it together. You know, a party sitting there in our fluffy robes. Linda's appointment was the first of the day, then mine, and then Kris'. However, I got there first, so they took me first. Linda scowled. My plan? In, out, done! Get home and start work on Thanksgiving stuff.

Not the plan. The mammogram showed something "concerning", that was the doctor's word. They needed more images, then an ultrasound and finally a biopsy. The phone call came from the doctor, cancer. Next came an MRI, two days later a second MRI, another biopsy, and another phone call, more cancer. Surgery.

And what's crazy was that Linda was also diagnosed with cancer. We both had major surgery to cut away all the tissue that was threatening us.

Did that mean we had somehow missed God's blessing? Not at all, because God walked with us every step of the way. God's presence was all over this and He has used it as a testimony to His faithfulness.

When the Bible speaks of blessing it means something way bigger than the stuff of the here and now. Our health can fail, our finances can take a nosedive, our prosperity could someday disappear. And even though all those things are critically important to God, it isn't the real blessing. The real blessing, the thing that the world can never touch, and it can never be snatched away, is knowing God. There is nothing in life more blessed, more rewarding, and more secure.

The book of Revelation promises a blessing. And even more than that, it is a three-fold blessing.

"Blessed is the one who reads aloud the words of this prophecy, and blessed are those who hear it and take to heart what is written in it, because the time is near." Revelation 1:3

We are blessed when we read it. We are blessed when we hear it. We are blessed when we believe and obey it. That's a lot of blessing. And all of it is available at every moment of every day, no matter what is happening around us.

As we close for today, have a blessed day!

DAY 4

"Are we there yet?"

"When will it be my birthday?"

"How many more days till Christmas?"

If we have spent much time around children, we've heard those questions. They want to know when the special events in their lives are going to happen. But this isn't just children; it's actually in all of us to want to know the dates and the time.

And so, the question arises, "Are we there yet?"

Is the time, when the book of Revelation reaches its fulfillment, near?

With our world changing every day, it is a question being raised. Is the time of the end near? Of course, we want to know.

And the answer is, "Yes!"

Revelation 1:3 says: *"Blessed is the one who reads aloud the words of this prophecy, and blessed are those who hear it and take to heart what is written in it, because the time is near."*

Notice the last few words of this verse, *"because the time is near".*

John was instructed to write down the words of this book 2000 years ago. The Revelation was given for blessing and encouragement and to be faith building for all the generations that would follow. It is for us today.

It was near then. So, it stands to reason that it is much nearer now.

As we look around, we can see that the world is set up for the fulfillment. Some are calling for a global government. We have technology that will allow us to buy and sell in a cashless society. The use of artificial intelligence is growing as we speak. All of these are signs that what was written 2000 years ago is so much nearer now.

But be assured of this, God knows the exact right time, and all of this is in His hands. When we know Him, we can trust Him with our days and our future.

The book opens with this greeting: *"John, To the seven churches in the province of Asia: Grace and peace to you…" Revelation 1:4*

This book is addressed to churches. If we are believers, then we are the church, and this message is for us. So, we need to pay special attention.

The seven churches that John was writing to at the time were in Asia Minor. The church was under great persecution. There was uncertainty and fear. It was a time of trouble and pain.

But look at the first words given to the churches: grace and peace.

We are living in times of change and uncertainty, fear, trouble, and pain. But this message is also for us: grace and peace.

Grace was the greeting of the Greeks. It's a big word.

I heard these definitions years ago:

Justice is getting what we deserve.

Mercy is not getting what we deserve.

But grace is getting what we don't deserve.

It doesn't just involve forgiveness for wrongs that we have committed. Grace goes way beyond that. It means gifts that we haven't in any way earned and certainly don't deserve. Grace is unmerited favor. And yet, grace is what God extends to us when we come to Him in repentance and receive the gift of salvation. Grace comes first, and then there is peace.

Peace was the greeting of the Jews. You still hear it today, "Shalom!" It's a beautiful word that is so much more than not having conflict or strife. It is a peace that goes beyond our ability to understand. It's being wrapped in the arms of the Lord in spite of conflict and strife and sheltered in the storm. He is the God of all Grace and the Prince of Peace. He is the place where we find both grace and peace.

There is chaos in our world, but when we know the Lord, the promise for us today and every day is grace and peace. God's unmerited favor and shalom!

The verse continues, *"John, To the seven churches in the province of Asia: Grace and peace to you from him who is, and who was, and who is to come, and from the seven spirits before his throne, and from Jesus Christ, who is the faithful witness, the firstborn from the dead, and the ruler of the kings of the earth..." Revelation 1:4-5*

This greeting of grace and peace is not just from John. The grace and peace are from God the Father, the Son, and the Holy Spirit. It is God's desire for us to experience abundant, unfathomable grace, and overwhelming peace. There is not only a three-fold blessing in these verses; there is a three-fold signature.

When someone says we have their word on something, we trust that they will do it. Right here we have the Word of the Father, the Son, and the Holy Spirit. There is nothing more trustworthy than that. We unequivocally have His Word on it.

"...To him who loves us and has freed us from our sins by his blood, and has made us to be a kingdom and priests to serve his God and Father—to him be glory and power forever and ever! Amen." Revelation 1:5-6

Look at what these verses say belongs to us when we know and follow the Lord.

He loves us. We are loved and valued and treasured by the Creator and Sustainer of this whole planet. We get to walk in that love.

He has freed us from our sins. When Adam and Eve ate the fruit in the Garden of Eden, it was one sin. And yet, the price for that one single sin was death. Sin and death entered the world.

In Isaiah 53 we read that all of us like sheep have gone astray. We all have that stain of sin on our hearts. I was changing channels the other night and heard a woman crying out these words, "I just wish I could get rid of these stains that are on my heart." Jesus is the way to have those stains removed.

The Bible tells us that God laid on Him the iniquity, the sin, the unrighteousness of us all. Jesus took every one of our sins on Him. He went to the cross. He died. He paid the price. He took our punishment. His body was placed in the grave. But then, and this is such good news, death couldn't hold Him. He rose. He conquered our sin. The price for one sin was death. If there had been one single sin that He couldn't forgive, death would have kept Him in the grave. But He rose. Because of that beautiful, amazing, magnificent Resurrection Sunday, the world had a Savior.

We have a Savior.

And He offers the cleansing and forgiveness and freedom to us all. It is a free gift. We need only repent and receive His offer of salvation.

Then, on top of all that, He brings us into His Kingdom. We become royalty, joint heirs with Christ. And we also become priests, those who have access to His presence and get to live out the high calling and privilege of serving.

Loved, treasured, cleansed, forgiven, made to be kings, and made to be priests.

It is a glorious calling. It is a magnificent calling.

DAY 5

Every year I look forward to the return of spring. Crocuses bloom, daffodils lift their heads, tulips join the party, and trees burst forth in colorful splendor. It feels like a breath of fresh air, and maybe that's because it is.

And then, after the heat of summer, I long for the return to cooler fall days and the moment when the leaves pull out all the stops and emerge with their breathtaking brightly colored foliage.

November arrives and I look forward to Thanksgiving with its family gatherings and abundant food.

And we can't forget Christmas. What a wonderful blessing that Christmas returns every year. The lights, the sounds, the smells, the festive air, the excitement in the eyes of children, all of these are things we look forward to.

It's wonderful that God gives us beautiful events. Each year we anticipate their return, but they all pale in comparison to a "return" that is on the horizon, an event that will absolutely take place one of these days.

It is the return of Jesus Christ to the earth. It's called the Second Coming.

"Look, he is coming with the clouds,' and 'every eye will see him, even those who pierced him'; and all peoples on earth 'will mourn because of him.' So shall it be! Amen. 'I am the Alpha and the Omega,' says the Lord God, 'who is, and who was, and who is to come, the Almighty.'" Revelation 1:7-8

Jesus is coming. He's coming! One of these days Jesus is returning to earth. This is a return for which there is no comparison. It is on the horizon. It is on God's timetable. It is going to happen.

For many it will be the joyful fulfillment of all their dreams. But there will also be mourning. This says ALL peoples on earth will mourn.

Why?

Now, we can only speculate, but for believers, when His righteousness and purity are revealed, will there be moments of mourning and regret over sin? In Christ, our sin has absolutely been forgiven, washed away, and God has forgotten it, but we still remember. There are times in our lives now when we look back with regret and pain and wish we hadn't done some of what we have done. Will it also be that there will be regret over what more could have been done to serve our glorious Lord? Wasted time, wasted opportunities, and grief over those who don't know the Lord. Certainly, all of that would cause us to mourn. However, that will last but a moment because He will wipe away every tear.

But there will be those who have never made a commitment to the Lord. Jesus Christ is pure love, pure peace, pure joy. People will one day realize they missed Jesus, and with that will come great mourning and weeping for what could have been. And that mourning will last for eternity.

There is still time to choose.

DAY 6

"I, John, your brother and companion in the suffering and kingdom and patient endurance that are ours in Jesus, was on the island of Patmos because of the word of God and the testimony of Jesus." Revelation 1:9

How much have I suffered for the cause of Christ? If I'm being honest, not much at all. John, however, did suffer. He was persecuted, exiled, and it really was because of his faith. He was taken to Patmos because of the Word of God and his testimony of Jesus.

Being a follower of Christ, being a believer, being one who serves the Lord, doesn't guarantee that we will be free from persecution, or suffering, or challenging times. In fact, Jesus said in *John 16:33, "I have told you these things, so that in me you may have peace. In this world you will have trouble. But take heart! I have overcome the world."*

In this world, we will have trouble. It feels like that right now, doesn't it? Trouble seems to be on lots of fronts.

The news is unsettling.

The economy is unsettling.

Impending storms are unsettling.

Health scares are unsettling.

It feels like trouble is sometimes pounding at the front door or creeping in through the backdoor.

However, the promise from Jesus' own lips is that, when trouble comes, in Him we can have peace.

And we can pray for our families, churches, neighbors, leaders, our city, our nation, and the world. No matter how trouble comes, Jesus has overcome the world.

John was suffering on the island of Patmos and then…"*On the Lord's Day I was in the Spirit…" Revelation 1:10*

John was in exile. He was away from his church body. He couldn't hang out with his friends. He didn't have access to any kind of encouraging Christian fellowship or extra Bible teaching. John was by himself. He was walking this path alone.

And yet, he was never alone. The Lord was with Him. He could enter the presence of Almighty God at any moment of any day and nothing, NOTHING, could stop him.

Trials, challenges, difficulties in our lives cannot stop our fellowship with God. Every minute of every day we have immediate access to the throne room. We can walk right into the presence of God, and His presence never leaves us. Never are we alone. Never ever, even for one moment, are we by ourselves when we are in Christ.

And not only was John not alone, but *"On the Lord's Day I was in the Spirit, and I heard behind me a loud voice like a trumpet…" Revelation 1:10*

John heard the Lord's voice. In exile, as a prisoner, in the stripped-down version of his life, John could still hear the voice.

And perhaps removing distractions from our lives can help us to hear.

Have you ever heard God speak? He does want to communicate with us. In John 10, Jesus reminds us that His sheep hear His voice.

He doesn't always speak exactly the same way. God walked with Adam and Eve in the cool of the evening. The Lord appeared to Abraham at his tent to tell him that he and Sarah would have a child in a year. Moses saw a burning bush and out of that came the voice of God. The children of Israel heard a trumpet blast and the thunderings from Mt. Sinai. God spoke to Elijah in a whisper. On Patmos John heard a loud voice like a trumpet.

It sounds lovely, doesn't it, hearing the voice of God?

So how does He speak today? One way we know for sure is through His Word. One of the wonderful blessings of having the Scripture is that we can hear His voice anytime. We need only pick up the Bible and read. Someone has said that if we want to hear God speak audibly, we should simply read the Bible out loud.

What a blessed day we live in. We always have access to His Word. It's on our phones, our computers; we have hard copies on our bookshelves.

We miss hearing Him when we don't take the time to listen.

Allow time to focus on hearing from the Lord. Listen for His voice. What words of encouragement and tender reminders of His love and faithfulness does He offer? Pick up the Bible and see.

He loves to speak to us.

DAY 7

Starting a new job can be challenging; the learning curve can seem too steep.

"On the Lord's Day I was in the Spirit, and I heard behind me a loud voice like a trumpet, which said: 'Write on a scroll what you see and send it to the seven churches: to Ephesus, Smyrna, Pergamum, Thyatira, Sardis, Philadelphia and Laodicea.'" Revelation 1:10-11

This was a new job. It was a big assignment and John was an old guy. He was in exile. He was a prisoner. He had a whole lot of reasons why he couldn't take on a new job. He could have come up with some excuses for not doing this. And yet, he didn't. God was about to take John on the biggest joy-filled-ride any person on the planet would ever experience. He was getting an all-expense-paid trip to view heaven and to gaze into the future. Just think about what he would have missed if he had asked God to pick someone else.

God has jobs for every one of us to do. The calling of God continues even during difficult circumstances. We have been brought into the Kingdom for such a time as this.

When God calls, how will we respond and what will we miss if we come up with excuses for why we can't do it?

Lord, please help us to say, "Yes," to You when You call.

"I turned around to see the voice that was speaking to me. And when I turned I saw seven golden lampstands, and among the lampstands was someone like a son of man, dressed in a robe reaching down to his feet and with a golden sash around his chest." Revelation 1:12-13

John turned around...

He was looking one direction but suddenly had to turn.

What direction are we looking? There are times in our lives when we need to stop, look, evaluate, and turn around.

In the Old Testament, one of the Hebrew words for repentance means to turn. We turn from sin and turn toward the Lord.

Let's ask ourselves some questions.

Is there anything in my life that needs to be changed?

How can I better serve the Lord?

What part of me needs to turn?

The voice was speaking to John. The voice is speaking to us. Am I listening?

But the great beauty of this is that when John did turn around, he saw. He saw the Lord. Jesus was right there with him. Oh, how I want that in my life. I want to see Jesus more clearly, more closely, more intimately. I want to see Him.

"I turned around to see the voice that was speaking to me. And when I turned I saw seven golden lampstands, and among the lampstands was someone like a son of man, dressed in a robe reaching down to his feet and with a golden sash around his chest. The hair on his head was white like wool, as white as snow, and his eyes were like blazing fire. His feet were like bronze glowing in a furnace, and his voice was like the sound of rushing waters. In his right hand he held seven stars, and coming out of his mouth was a sharp, double-edged sword. His face was like the sun shining in all its brilliance." Revelation 1:12-16

The Gospels don't record Jesus' height, weight, color of his hair. We don't have a physical description of Him. However, we do read in Isaiah 53 that Messiah had no beauty or majesty to attract us to Him. It wasn't Jesus' looks that drew people. It was His love and mercy and grace.

But here in these few verses in Revelation, we are given a brief glimpse of Him.

He was dressed similarly to the priests when they went into the Temple to serve. Only the High Priest could go into the holiest part of the Temple. Jesus is our great High Priest. 1 Timothy 2:5 tells us that He is the mediator between God and man.

Jesus' hair was white like wool. He is the Lamb of God.

His eyes were like blazing fire.

I am stopping here to ask a question, when do my eyes blaze? Because most of the time, they don't. However, if anyone ever attempts to hurt one of my children or grandchildren, they will definitely see eyes blazing with fire. And perhaps that's one of the reasons why Jesus' eyes are blazing, because there are people suffering and under persecution. There is injustice and unrighteousness in our world.

His feet were like bronze glowing in a furnace. What a reminder that He was that fourth Man in the fiery furnace when Shadrach, Meshach, and Abednego stood for their faith and faced the fire. He is with us through all of life's fiery trials.

And His voice was like the sound of rushing waters. If you have ever been to Niagara Falls or another of earth's rushing waters, you know that the sound of that water drowns out all other sounds. His voice, if we will listen, drowns out all other voices. And even when He whispers, it is the biggest voice in the world.

His face was like the sun shining in all its brilliance. The Shekinah Glory radiates out of Messiah.

What a beautiful portrait.

John used the word "like" over and over. Like a son of man, eyes like blazing fire, feet like bronze, a voice like rushing waters, His face like the sun, those comparisons are for our benefit. The presence was so great that there aren't words big enough to use to describe the glory, the magnificence, the majesty, the beauty, the splendor of our Savior.

John saw Jesus.

Someday, so will we.

"… and coming out of his mouth was a sharp, double-edged sword…"
Revelation 1:16

This one phrase is so powerful. A sword, a double-edged sword, was coming out of His mouth. Ephesians 6:17 tells us that the sword of the Spirit is the Word of God. Hebrews 4:12 says the Word of God is living, sharper than any double-edged sword.

Out of the mouth of Jesus is the Word of God and a double-edged sword means it cuts both ways. So, both sides are true.

Jesus is the beginning. He is the end.

He is the Alpha and the Omega.

He is the first and the last.

He is fully man. He is fully God.

He is our Great High Priest. He is also the perfect sacrifice.

He is the Bread of Life. He is the Living Water.

He is the Lion of Judah. He is the Lamb of God.

He is our friend. He is our rabbi.

He is judge over the world. He is our advocate.

He is the King of Kings. He is the suffering servant.

He is the Good Shepherd who guards the sheepfold.

He is the Lamb who takes away the sin of the world.

He bore the curse for sin. He is the cure for sin.

He is the cornerstone. He is the capstone.

He is the root. He is the branch.

He is the Creator. He is the sustainer.

He is the author. He is the finisher.

He was dead. He is alive.

He is the one who was, who is, and who is to come.

He is the beginning. He is the end and everything in between.

He is the great I AM.

DAY 8

"*When I saw him, I fell at his feet as though dead…*" *Revelation 1:17*

John knew Jesus. He walked with Him. He ate meals with Him. He was one of Jesus' disciples. For three and a half years he was by the Savior's side. He was one of only three chosen to be with the Lord on the Mount of Transfiguration. He was sitting next to Jesus at the Passover. John was right there at the crucifixion. Jesus gave him the honor of caring for Mary, His mother. John was at the grave. He saw the resurrected Messiah. He stood on the Mount of Olives as Jesus ascended into heaven. As much as any man could, John knew Jesus.

And yet, this magnificent revelation of Jesus overwhelmed him to the point of death.

This was a heavenly vision of the Creator of the Universe and even though John knew Him so well, his face hit the dirt.

John fell prostrate before the Lord, but Jesus didn't leave John on the ground as if he were dead.

"*…Then he placed his right hand on me and said: 'Do not be afraid. I am the First and the Last. I am the Living One; I was dead, and now look, I am alive for ever and ever! And I hold the keys of death and Hades.'*" *Revelation 1:17-18*

This moment of fear was replaced with the gentle touch of the Savior. He reached out His right hand and spoke these sweet words, *"Do not be afraid."*

Jesus doesn't want us to be afraid. His Revelation might overwhelm us. His presence might be more than we can take in, but His words are of a Gentle Shepherd soothing away any anxiety, fear, terror.

Our dear Savior is reaching out His hand to us with those same sweet words today and every day, *"Do not be afraid."*

John was Jesus' beloved friend. When he saw the Lord, he fell prostrate before Him. He saw the awesome majesty of the reigning Lord and the response was to fall on his face.

Throughout Scripture we see people who dared to stand against the Lord.

Throughout history there have been people who dared to stand against the Lord.

There are people who believe that in eternity they will dare to stand against the Lord.

That will not happen.

When the heavenly intersects with the earthly, we puny humans cower. Over and over in the Bible, we see that even when God sent an angel, the first response was fear. So, the heavenly messenger began with, "Don't be afraid."

But here, this was not an encounter with an angel. This was an encounter with the Lord.

Philippians 2:9-11, "Therefore God exalted him to the highest place and gave him the name that is above every name, that at the name of Jesus every knee should bow, in heaven and on earth and under the earth, and every tongue acknowledge that Jesus Christ is Lord, to the glory of God the Father."

Every single person on the planet will someday bow before Jesus.

We have the privilege, the joy of starting now.

DAY 9

John was in exile, a prison camp. The physical world where he lived would have been trying, difficult. One day followed the next, a very hard, meager, challenging life. What beauty did he see on that rock? What encouragement did he receive from other people? What fellowship did he have?

But God didn't leave him with only the mundane, the stripped-down version of a life. God gave John the gift of a lifetime. He opened heaven. He revealed Himself. He gave John a glorious, magnificent, overwhelming vision of Himself.

But God didn't leave John there either, just basking in the glory of seeing Jesus. The Lord then gave him an assignment, a job, a place to serve. *"Write, therefore, what you have seen, what is now and what will take place later." Revelation 1:19*

John needed the vision, but he also needed to serve the Lord.

We can, at any moment, see Christ when we open His Word. There are times when we are reduced to tears at the beauty of who He is and what He has done. We get to see through John's eyes this vision. We can feel Jesus wrap His arms around us and hear Him whisper to us not to be afraid.

But stepping out of the mundane into the sublime isn't enough for us either. God calls all of us to serve. He has assignments for every day. He wants to use us in the Kingdom. So, God gifts us all differently. There are preachers, evangelists, teachers, missionaries, worship leaders, people who work with children, teenagers, adults. There are those called to be up-front. There are those called to be behind the scenes. There are many ways to serve.

But there is one job to which we are all called, and that is to pray.

I am convinced that prayer is one of the biggest things we can do in the Kingdom. Prayer crosses all physical barriers. I am praying right now for anyone reading this book. Our lives right now may be separated by distance, but God sees and moves in all directions.

Prayer crosses time. We can pray for people in the world today to know the Lord. We can pray for future generations to know the Lord.

Prayer doesn't require any talent or great ability on our part and there are no age restrictions. God hears the cry of the tiniest child, the feeblest senior, the most educated scholar, or those with little or no education. Our age, abilities, giftedness, or status do not play a part in God hearing our prayers.

Prayer costs nothing. No special wardrobe or equipment is needed.

And no circumstance, no event, no object, no one can stop us from praying. We can all pray.

And then, of course, God also gives us opportunities to serve in other capacities.

He may just give the assignment, "Write".

DAY 10

"*Write, therefore, what you have seen, what is now and what will take place later.*" *Revelation 1:19*

John was told to write what he had seen, what was happening at that moment, and then what would take place later. In other words, write what was, what is, and what is to come.

Scholars have dubbed this verse, "the divine outline." I like that. It's easy to remember the outline of the book.

What was. What had John just seen? In chapter 1, John experienced an encounter with the Lord Jesus. He saw Him in His glory and splendor and was told to write that down. What a blessing for us; we get to see through John's eyes this glimpse of Jesus' beauty and majesty. We get to have the assurance that He is alive and reigning.

What is. Chapters 2 and 3 are what was taking place right then. These two chapters are messages to seven churches in Asia Minor. They were real churches during John's lifetime and the message was for them. But these are also messages for us today. Chapters 2 and 3 of this book are so very important for the church in the modern world. What does God commend? What does he condemn? What does He challenge us to do? What does He caution us to stay away from?

What is to come. Then God told John to write down what will take place later. In chapter 4, John was suddenly caught up to the throne room of God. Heaven was opened. There were angels worshiping, elders bowing, and the music and songs of eternity.

This is glorious and as believers this will someday be our experience also. There is coming a day when heaven will be opened for all of us, and we will be transported to the presence of Almighty God. The apostle Paul reminds us that it hasn't even entered our minds the wonderfulness that awaits us. As big and awesome and grand that we can think about in our minds doesn't begin to touch the reality.

And then, beginning in chapter 6 of this marvelous book, God lifts the veil on the future and gives us a glimpse of earth's last days. What a wonderful gift God has given to the entire world. Every one of us can look now and see what lies ahead and then choose.

Who will we follow?

What was, what is, and what is to come, what a gift!

DAY 11

The King James Version of Revelation 1:1 says, *"The Revelation of Jesus Christ, which God gave unto him, to shew unto his servants things which must shortly come to pass; and he sent and signified it by his angel unto his servant John:"*

God's signature is all over this book. God alone knows every inch, every second of future events. Only He could have written this. Prophecy is one of the proofs that God is the author of the Scripture.

But that word "signified" also helps us to see that much of the book is written in signs. When we read Revelation, we see lots of images, allusions, similes, metaphors, and signs for us to discover.

So why? Why use images and signs? Let's examine that.

First, they are descriptive. For example, the word beast says way more than the word dictator. A dictator can be malevolent, but he could also possibly be benevolent. But beast? That speaks of evil and harm and awfulness. We get a way bigger picture of who this global leader will be with that image. So, a picture can be worth a thousand words.

Secondly, language can be fluid. The meaning of words can change over time. But a beast is still a beast today, a seed is a seed, a serpent is still a serpent.

So, this book is filled with pictures we need to examine to understand.

When John first saw the vision of Christ in Revelation 1:12, Jesus was standing among seven lampstands. He held in His right hand seven stars. Stars, lampstands? What do those mean?

Part of the beauty of this Book is that not only does God give the images and signs; He gives the definitions. Some of those definitions will be tucked away in the Revelation. However, for some we will have to go on a hunt through the Old Testament. But a hunt through the Scripture leads to treasure. So, as we walk through this Book, we will be on an amazing treasure hunt.

Verse 12 introduced the stars and the lampstands, but here in verse 20, God explains them.

"The mystery of the seven stars that you saw in my right hand and of the seven golden lampstands is this: The seven stars are the angels of the seven churches, and the seven lampstands are the seven churches." Revelation 1:20

Ah, discovery. God really wants us to understand. But I also think He wants us to enjoy the thrill of finding the treasure.

Get ready, there is so much more on this treasure hunt.

REVELATION
CHAPTER 2

DAY 12

Now we're going to walk into chapter 2 of Revelation. So, how are we doing? Is this scary or frightening? Or have you begun to feel the grace and peace that God wants us to experience in this wonderful Book? Knowing Christ and walking with Him is the way to be absolutely certain that we always have access to that rest.

A crime hit the national news. It included a child, kidnapping, supposed violence. It turned out to be completely contrived and no one knows exactly why. It's pretty hard sometimes to know what and who to trust.

Our world is changing. Right is proclaimed as wrong and wrong is embraced as right. Yes, we are living in very uncertain times. But the Word of God is a place we can go, and every day find the reliability of truth.

For right now, let's set aside the stuff of the world and look at one of the beautiful pictures that Revelation gives us of our Savior and the world He promises. It brings into focus Jesus as our Bridegroom. Some people want to run from the book of Revelation. We find it more comforting than the best home cooked meal or being wrapped in our favorite sherpa throw. This book proclaims that Jesus is in charge. He's got this! He's coming as our Groom.

I want you to think for a moment about how much a waiting groom longs to see the face of his bride. He is anxiously anticipating her arrival. He only has eyes for her as he looks down the aisle for his first glimpse. The love he has for her is evident on his face.

The church is the bride of Christ. One of the things we need to remember is our Groom loves us with a love so intense that we cannot even imagine it. The picture of the bride and groom is just that, a picture. The reality is completely beyond our present understanding. What a marvelous event we have to look forward to.

He will do everything to protect and provide for us, even in uncertain times. He is here for us. We don't have to be afraid.

"To the angel of the church in Ephesus write: These are the words of him who holds the seven stars in his right hand and walks among the seven golden lampstands." Revelation 2:1

He holds the seven stars in His right hand. Do you see this? He is so powerful that all these churches are held in one hand. And don't you just love that!

No matter what the church faces, He is protecting us, providing for us, and above all, loving us.

Rejoice church, your Bridegroom is holding you in His hand. What a difference that makes!

Each of the churches listed in Revelation 2-3 was a literal congregation in Asia Minor. But one of the amazing truths about this list is that they most likely also represent church ages that have taken place throughout history. In any other order, this would not be the case. So, there are lessons to learn from church history, but there are also lessons to learn from each of these congregations for us today.

Ephesus is the first church listed. Some of the meanings for the name Ephesus can be desired one or beloved. This points to how much Jesus loves the church. Historically this would have been the church age at the time of the apostles.

"I know your deeds, your hard work and your perseverance. I know that you cannot tolerate wicked people, that you have tested those who claim to be apostles but are not, and have found them false. You have persevered and have endured hardships for my name, and have not grown weary." Revelation 2:2-3

This church had a lot of their priorities in the correct order. They were hard workers, recognized wickedness and refused to stand for it, understood truth, and persevered. They would not grow weary and quit. The Lord had a lot of good to say to them.

And don't we want that? We want to hear that we are pleasing Him. What can we learn from this church?

Work hard...look for ways to make a difference.

Persevere...keep on, even in difficult circumstances.

Refuse to tolerate wickedness...don't accept every teaching, but test it through the Word of God.

Endure hardships...recognize that the Lord can use everything for building His Kingdom.

Don't quit because things get difficult...we have news for you, they will!

The Lord had a lot of good to say to this church, but His message wasn't over.

Uh oh!

"I hold this against you..."

These few words from the mouth of God are chilling.

Think about it. You're reading a note or having a conversation and suddenly you receive a message that begins like this: "Yet I hold this against you..."

Wow. What a statement and this is from God, Himself. He is the One saying that He has something against this church at Ephesus. So, what is He saying?

"You have forsaken the love you had at first." Revelation 2:4

There was a time when this church had greater love for God, for one another, for reaching the world with the message.

They lost that first, all-encompassing, all-consuming love that broke through everything else. It wasn't that it wasn't attainable. They drifted from it. They allowed that love to cool and something else became more important.

Uh oh!

Let's take an inventory.

Has there been a time in our lives when our love for Jesus was stronger than it is today?

If the answer is yes, then we need to pay attention. There is an important message ahead.

Alright, let's look at this verse again.

"Yet I hold this against you: You have forsaken the love you had at first." Revelation 2:4

Busyness, or when things come to a screeching boring halt, the cares of this world, difficult or trying circumstances that we have no control over, slipping into the comfort of the day-to-day, allowing a bit of yeast to creep into our hearts, and a myriad of other things can all contribute to a love that cools and gets stale.

But there is a remedy for this challenge that the Lord has given.

"Consider how far you have fallen! Repent and do the things you did at first. If you do not repent, I will come to you and remove your lampstand from its place." Revelation 2:5

Repent and do.

First, let's take an assessment. We need to ask ourselves how far we have fallen. Where were we and where are we now? We need to be honest. If we are not in that love we had at first, what took us away?

Whatever it is, the message is clear. Repent. Turn around, don't walk. Run! Run right into the arms of the Savior. Confess it all to Him.

The bottom line is that we must own it. We don't make excuses, blame others, minimize. We admit our sins to the Lord and ask Him to forgive us. He promises us He will. He wipes the slate completely clean.

Then the mandate is to do. Do the things we did at first. In our earthly relationships, love equals time. If we want to grow in love, we have to spend time together. It's the same for our spiritual lives; we must spend time with the Lord.

Read the Bible. We can wrap ourselves up in His wonderful Word, breathing in the sweetness.

Pray. We can spend time basking in the sunlight of His presence, immersing ourselves in love and brightness and enjoying our walk with Him. We can become very serious about our prayer life and determine to do battle on our knees.

Meet with other Christians. Other believers spur us on to love and good deeds. We need the church.

Share the Gospel. Seeing a baby born is one of life's grandest moments. Seeing someone born into the Kingdom is one of eternity's grandest moments.

Sing praises to the Lord. Psalm 22:3 helps us understand that God inhabits the praises of His people. He is right here with us when we open our hearts in worship and praise and honor and adoration.

In other words, we must be busy in the Kingdom. Being in His Word and in His presence, causes us to fall more in love with Him.

Here is the command:

"Repent and do the things you did at first!"

DAY 13

Jesus was speaking to the church at Ephesus and informed them, that in the church, there are practices to applaud and there are practices to hate.

"But you have this in your favor: You hate the practices of the Nicolaitans, which I also hate." Revelation 2:6

Wait, did we read that right? "Hate!" God uses the word hate?

I remember sometimes as I was teaching that a well-meaning student would decide that it was his or her duty to keep me informed about the language of another child. Sometimes the report would begin with, "Teacher, he said a bad word. He said 'hate'." And that opened the door for me to do some teaching on things to hate and things we must not hate.

This passage makes it clear to us that there are things to hate.

This passage is clear that it was appropriate to hate the practices of the Nicolaitans. The Nicolaitans were a sect, promoting a religious teaching that mixed the world into the relationship with Jesus, saying you could live any way you wanted.

The Bible tells us that God is the judge, and we will all someday stand before Him. He has given us His Word and Scripture outlines what is right and what is wrong. The Word of God is the tool that we use to determine whether certain practices are okay. It is not the desire of the person, the bent of a nation, the path of society. The benchmark is the Word of God.

The word hate is not used loosely. It is a very powerful Greek word. It means to abhor, find completely repulsive.

But let's be clear, the Word does not say Jesus hated the Nicolaitans, it says He hated their practices.

When we come to Jesus, there are things we need to confess and leave at the cross. We are called to live a holy, separated life. The Nicolaitans were embracing heresy, immorality, and idolatry even though the Lord had said, "No".

They were wrong and Jesus said He hated what they were doing, because He knows that sin ultimately destroys. He hates the sin but loves the people.

So should we.

And then Jesus ends this message to the church in Ephesus with a challenge that has rung through the ages. It is for all of us.

"Whoever has ears, let them hear what the Spirit says to the churches. To the one who is victorious, I will give the right to eat from the tree of life, which is in the paradise of God." Revelation 2:7

It was written for them. It is written for us. Do we have ears? If the answer is yes, the command is to live victoriously. Let's choose to live in victory.

DAY 14

I began to share the Gospel with a young woman after a church service. She was very offended, got up, and stormed out. I was stunned, wondering what I had done to make her so angry. Frankly, I never saw her again. I beat myself up over that one. But what I have come to understand is that most people need to hear the story of salvation several times before committing their lives to Christ. Was I being persecuted as she yelled at me?

No, that wasn't persecution. That was a challenge. I'll be honest. I have never been persecuted for my faith.

This next church was.

"To the angel of the church in Smyrna write..." Revelation 2:8

Smyrna is the second church that the Lord addresses. They were facing great persecution. You can hear in the name Smyrna the root word myrrh. Myrrh is a death spice. In the Bible, we read that it was used as a part of the preparation of bodies for burial.

Why was this church facing persecution?

Belief in Christ began to spread. Many were becoming followers. But there were also many who became enemies, making it their single focus to wipe out the followers of Jesus.

We see in the book of Acts that Stephen was dragged before the Sanhedrin, questioned, but then taken out and stoned for his faith. I love what it tells us of his last moments. He looked up as the stones were pelting against him. *"'Look,' he said, 'I see heaven open and the Son of Man standing at the right hand of God.'" Acts 7:56*

We know from Hebrews 12:2 that when Jesus ascended into heaven, He sat down at the right hand of God. But look at what it says here in Acts. Stephen saw Him standing. What a welcome! As Stephen took his last breath here, Jesus stood up to welcome him home to take his first breath in heaven.

Stephen's death began a wave of persecution against believers that continues to this day.

Christians around the world face persecution. It is not over yet. But remember, as we take our last breath here, He will welcome us home to take our first breath there.

His message to this church continues. *"To the angel of the church in Smyrna write: These are the words of him who is the First and the Last, who died and came to life again." Revelation 2:8*

There is so much hope in these few words. "He is the First and the Last..."

What comfort. He was there at the beginning. He will be there at the end. He is there every day in-between. When I wake up in the morning, He greets me. When I close my eyes at night, He stands guard, rejoicing over me with singing. (Zephaniah 3:17)

Revelation 2:8 "…who died and came to life again."

Jesus was crucified. He gave up His life for us. He was buried and a stone was rolled and sealed in front of His death cave. But death was no match for His life. Early in the morning, He broke free from the curse of death and for all time, He lives. He is alive today.

It then becomes a promise for us. Yes, death will come, but we will live again. The church at Smyrna did not know when they would be taken by the enemy and face death. Jesus was promising them that He was bigger than death. Jesus promises us that He is bigger than death.

We are living in uncertain times.

Remember, Jesus is bigger than uncertain times, bigger than difficult circumstances. Jesus is bigger than death.

No matter what we face He has great encouragement for us. *"I know your afflictions and your poverty—yet you are rich! I know about the slander of those who say they are Jews and are not, but are a synagogue of Satan." Revelation 2:9*

The Lord knew what the church of Smyrna was going through. He knew the state of their finances. He knew their afflictions. But He told them they were rich because they knew Him.

He knows what we are going through. He knows the afflictions in our world. He knows the state of our finances. Real wealth does not come from what we have, it comes from Who we know. All our stuff will someday be gone. Our bank accounts, our cars, our houses, all the things that we can touch will come to an end and fade into dust. What is permanent is our relationship with Jesus Christ. Asking Him into our lives gives us the real wealth we need.

Knowing Jesus makes us rich forever.

DAY 15

What makes us afraid? I'm not afraid of spiders. I picked up a scorpion off a bathroom floor while visiting in the south. I don't worry about snakes when I'm out West. But you won't catch me trying on hats or using someone else's hairbrush because the idea of head lice about paralyzes me.

Fear. It is a genuine emotion. And different things make us afraid.

As we look at Smyrna, fear should have been prevalent for the early church, because persecution was rampant. People were arrested and killed for their faith.

But God has this encouraging word for the church in Smyrna. *"Do not be afraid of what you are about to suffer. I tell you, the devil will put some of you in prison to test you, and you will suffer persecution for ten days. Be faithful, even to the point of death, and I will give you life as your victor's crown." Revelation 2:10*

Do not be afraid; be faithful. How comforting those words would have been to this church. And those words still apply to us. Do not be afraid; be faithful.

It is our calling. It means we spend time in God's Word, we pray, we praise, we share truth, we look for opportunities to encourage, we bring joy even in the middle of difficult circumstances. We live out Jesus Christ.

The world has little hope in the middle of a mess. We have Jesus, and He gives the opportunity to turn the mess into the message.

I love that it tells us that these messages to the churches are to those who have ears. It is the only criteria for those who are to receive this message. Let me ask you again, do you have ears?

If the answer is yes, then you need to listen. So, do I.

"Whoever has ears, let them hear what the Spirit says to the churches. The one who is victorious will not be hurt at all by the second death." Revelation 2:11

A goal is presented here. Jesus is telling us to live a victorious life. But how do we do that?

It begins with knowing Jesus. We must come to the place where we recognize that we are sinners and need to invite Christ into our lives.

We must align ourselves with His Word. Spending time in Scripture gives us the tools we need to know where to place our feet.

We need to make prayer a part of our lives. We talk with those we love. We love Jesus so we need to have a running conversation with Him.

Do we have ears?

We need to listen!

DAY 16

Pergamum was in sharp contrast to Smyrna. The church at Smyrna had little as far as resources. Pergamum was right smack in the middle of wealth. Both churches came under attack. Smyrna faced persecution. Pergamum faced prosperity.

"To the angel of the church in Pergamum write: These are the words of him who has the sharp, double-edged sword." Revelation 2:12

Pergamum was a capital city and stood in both splendor and pride because of it. It boasted an extensive library, holding upwards of 200,000 books, each written by hand. Beautiful architecture enhanced the landscape, making this a magnificent city. It was a center of both emperor and idol worship. Temples were everywhere. Every type of idol worship was embraced and encouraged. And yet right in the middle of that pagan pandemic, God called a group of followers of Jesus Christ. He encouraged them that He is the One with the double-edged sword.

It was not an easy place to live out their faith but a place that desperately needed their faith.

Maybe your environment is a little like that...not an easy place to live out your faith but a place that desperately needs faith. Jesus is standing right here with a double-edged sword.

"For the word of God is alive and active. Sharper than any double-edged sword, it penetrates even to dividing soul and spirit, joints and marrow; it judges the thoughts and attitudes of the heart." Hebrews 4:12

The weapon described in this verse points to the Word of God. It cuts both ways. It rebukes and encourages. It challenges and comforts. It tells of the way to death but gives us the way to life. That life is in Jesus Christ.

But the lure for the church at Pergamum was to mix the world with their faith. Compromise is never the path to faithfulness.

A lot of sin can pollute, but a little sin can also pollute.

Pergamum had both, a little sin in some places and a lot in others. Both can be deadly.

"I know where you live—where Satan has his throne. Yet you remain true to my name. You did not renounce your faith in me, not even in the days of Antipas, my faithful witness, who was put to death in your city—where Satan lives." Revelation 2:13

Zeus was worshiped in Pergamum. A throne was erected to him that was so grand, about forty feet high. It could be seen all over the city and people traveled to worship there. It was certainly where Satan had his throne. There was great appeal in this city to worship the grand, the popular, the beautiful, the evil.

The church in Pergamum was not popular, and yet they remained true. Despite the lure to compromise, in spite of the persecution, the believers lived out their faith.

We must also.

DAY 17

We had a dog. She was a good dog. We got her as an adult rescue but had to change her name. She had been called Whiskey and we felt like it might be a little challenging to our testimony to stand outside and have the pastor and his wife yelling for whiskey. We wanted our words to line up with our actions and not let the neighbors think we were dying for a drink.

Pergamum was not matching their words with their actions.

We begin with a reference from Numbers 22. It starts with the prophet Balaam, who was offered a big reward by King Balak to pronounce a curse over God's people. At first, Balaam said, "No," but the prize money was increased, and he succumbed to the call. On the way, he was shown that he was on a path to his death because of his compromise. God only allowed him to continue when Balaam became convinced that cursing God's chosen nation was not the way to go.

At first, he spoke only words of affirmation over the Israelites, but even though his words were right, his heart was not. Because then, Balaam gave the enemy nation the roadmap to defeat Israel. He essentially told them to use this tactic, "If you can't beat them, join them." He outlined the compromise. And it worked. Israel fell right into the mess.

We see the same thing happening with Pergamum.

"Nevertheless, I have a few things against you: There are some among you who hold to the teaching of Balaam, who taught Balak to entice the Israelites to sin so that they ate food sacrificed to idols and committed sexual immorality." Revelation 2:14

We are to live according to the Word of God.

Some of the people at Pergamum compromised their integrity and complete commitment to the Lord. They allowed the lure of the world, the love for other things, and the lust for other people to take over their lives.

Satan has a roadmap to defeat. It includes compromise and immorality.

God has the roadmap to victory. It is to live out the Word of God.

But compromise had invaded Pergamum. The solution to that kind of compromise is listed here: *"Likewise, you also have those who hold to the teaching of the Nicolaitans. Repent therefore! Otherwise, I will soon come to you and will fight against them with the sword of my mouth."* Revelation 2:15-16

The call is, "Repent!"

So, let's take a mental walk through the rooms of our hearts and minds. If there is anything there that is calling us away from the Lord, we need to stop now, confess it, and ask the Lord to forgive us and wash it away.

He will. He loves to give us the opportunity to start fresh.

But we have a responsibility also. We must establish that relationship with Jesus Christ, but then fill our lives with Him through His Word and prayer.

"Whoever has ears, let them hear what the Spirit says to the churches. To the one who is victorious, I will give some of the hidden manna. I will also give that person a white stone with a new name written on it, known only to the one who receives it." Revelation 2:17

What hope we see in this verse. Promised to us is the hidden manna. It is the food that we need for these days. In Exodus God provided a special food for His children, but to get the manna, they had to pick it up. Our food too comes right from the hand of Almighty God and will sustain us. Our manna is the Word of God, but to get it, we have to pick it up.

And then He promises a new name.

No matter what our reputation has been…

No matter how sinful our past…

No matter who can point to us and say we're guilty of_____ (you fill in the blank), Jesus promises us a new start.

When we come to Him in repentance, He forgives us and pronounces a new name on us. It will be awarded to us on a white stone, and it comes from His hand.

No award, prize, trophy, or medal will ever compare. We will carry the name that He has chosen for each of us. It will be the name God calls us forever.

DAY 18

"To the angel of the church in…"

We are not certain who the text is referring to when it addresses the angel to each of the churches. The word angel means to announce, or to bring a message or to bring good news. So, there are some scholars who believe that these are literal angels protecting, guarding each congregation. That is a lovely thought. There are other scholars who believe that these are the pastors called to shepherd each of these churches. That is also a very lovely thought.

That means that the question of who these angels are is a bit of a debate.

I have to say that we can't know definitively either way. But I know this, they have a job to do. They are to be messengers to these people with the truth of God's Word. They are to deliver the message.

We are too. Could the Lord be calling us to act as angels to those around us? Are we to be delivering the message of hope, healing, salvation?

There is no debate that the answer to those questions is yes. We have a job to do.

The message to this next church begins: *"To the angel of the church in Thyatira write: These are the words of the Son of God, whose eyes are like blazing fire and whose feet are like burnished bronze."* Revelation 2:18

Thyatira was not nearly as large a city as Pergamum, but because it was on a major trade route, it was a thriving city. It was teeming with industry, trade, business. One of the industries that came from there was the color purple. This was a very expensive, but also a very lucrative business. The color could be derived from snails. It took thousands of them to harvest even a thimble full of dye. Purple was a color reserved for the rich and famous. Royalty was referred to as having been "born in the purple". It could also come from a plant called the madder root grown in this region. Both types were sought after and cherished.

Acts 16 tells us the account of a woman who heard the Gospel from Paul. She was from the city of Thyatira and was a dealer in purple, but when she heard the message, she responded. She most likely would have become a member of this church. Her name was Lydia.

She probably had everything the world could offer, but when she heard the truth of the Gospel, she responded. Her job in the world most likely meant prominence. But it wasn't until she met Jesus that her life was complete.

There is such a message here for us. Wealth, position, success mean very little without Jesus. But when we have Him, we have everything.

Let's read the affirmation that Jesus brings to this church at Thyatira, and then take an inventory to see how we're doing. We must remember that His message to each of the churches was for them, but it is also for us. *"I know your deeds, your love and faith, your service and perseverance, and that you are now doing more than you did at first." Revelation 2:19*

Okay, the deeds part. What are we doing right now to further the Kingdom?

Hmm, good question.

We can and should be praying. When we go out and see businesses or neighbors, we can remember to pray for them. We can pray for our families, our city, our state, our country.

We can be studying God's Word, going to church, joining Bible studies, listening to teaching online, on TV, or streaming services.

Next on the list is love and faith.

What is faith?

Faith is being sure of what we hope for and certain of what we do not see. Our eyes are not the determiner of what is really going on in our world. God is on the throne and completely in charge.

What is love?

Love can be shown, spoken, and written. It was best demonstrated when Jesus Christ willingly went to the cross to take our place and take the judgment for sin for the world.

And then, last on today's list is doing more than we did at first. We can praise, sing, pray, write, share, give, encourage...do more than we did at first.

"Nevertheless, I have this against you: You tolerate that woman Jezebel, who calls herself a prophet. By her teaching she misleads my servants into sexual immorality and the eating of food sacrificed to idols." Revelation 2:20

The reference to Jezebel goes back to the book of 1 Kings when a king named Ahab married a pagan woman named Jezebel. She brought idol worship, false prophets, immorality, and child sacrifice into the land of Israel, and God's chosen people began to embrace it. God was broken-hearted over it and sent prophets to speak against it.

But then centuries later a woman brought false teaching into the church at Thyatira. These same practices raised their ugly heads. And God was rebuking this church because they were tolerating it. *"Nevertheless, I have this against you..."*

That was a message for the church then. It is a message for the church today. Our call is to live according to the Word of God and not to be swayed by any teachings that contradict His Word. We are not to tolerate, accept, applaud, or embrace any false teaching within the church.

How do we identify false teaching? We study and memorize the Scripture, so we know the truth. Jesus loved people, but He did not tolerate the false teachings of the Pharisees and teachers of the law. He spoke the truth. We are called to speak truth.

Just like Jesus, we are all called to love people, and one of the most loving things we can do is to help people out of the bondage of sin with the truth of the Gospel message.

We are called to share truth and that brings freedom, and peace, and redemption, and joy, and...

DAY 19

When I was teaching, one of my strategies for helping a disobedient student to obey was to notice a classmate near them doing exactly what he or she was supposed to do. I would praise the child who was obeying. Then I would look to the other side of the misbehaving child and find another obedient classmate and shower the compliments. Sometimes acknowledging the right behavior caused the one going the wrong direction to pause, notice, and obey. It was giving him or her the time to come in under the blessing.

It is a little of what we see that God was doing with some of the people in the church at Thyatira. He began with praise for those who were following Him. But then He challenged and gave time for the others to turn away from their sin, turn to Him, setting the right direction.

But some refused to listen.

"I have given her time to repent of her immorality, but she is unwilling. So I will cast her on a bed of suffering, and I will make those who commit adultery with her suffer intensely, unless they repent of her ways. I will strike her children dead. Then all the churches will know that I am he who searches hearts and minds, and I will repay each of you according to your deeds." Revelation 2:21-23

We stop and ask the questions. Does God do that with us? Does God graciously give us time to take a serious look at our lives and reset the direction? Is this the moment to repent and follow Him? Not just for a few days or weeks but to make a life-altering, eternity-altering commitment to follow Him.

The answer to those questions is yes.

The church of Thyatira was given time to repent, but some refused. Their idol worship, immorality, and child sacrifice took them to a bed of suffering. God brought the punishment right back to where the sin began. Refusing to repent always eventually leads to suffering.

The message is clear. Repent while there is still time.

Let's remember that the churches in Revelation 2 and 3 were literal churches so the message was for them. There are messages in this for churches today. There are messages for each of us individually. But these churches are also symbolic of church history and seasons of time over the last two thousand years.

The name Thyatira has its root in the meaning of the word *sacrifice*. It was during this church season that a doctrine of continual sacrifice was introduced. It began to be taught that sin was not paid for once and for all but had to be paid for over and over again.

When Jesus was dying on the cross, He pronounced, "Tetelesti." It is translated as it is finished, but it also literally means paid in full. Our sin debt was paid by the only One who could pay it, Jesus Christ. When we come to Him, repent, ask Him to forgive us and come into our lives, He does. We have His Word on it. And then we are called to live according to His Word.

"Now I say to the rest of you in Thyatira, to you who do not hold to her teaching and have not learned Satan's so-called deep secrets, 'I will not impose any other burden on you, except to hold on to what you have until I come.'" Revelation 2:24-25

There we have it; we are to hold on to what we have until He comes. We are to hold on to the Word of God. We are to stay away from other teaching that can lead us astray or try to water down the power of God's truth. We can hold God's Word in our hands as we read it, in our minds as we memorize it, in our hearts as we sing it, in our faith as we immerse ourselves in it.

Hold on church! He is coming soon.

And then the prize comes.

"To the one who is victorious and does my will to the end, I will give authority over the nations—that one 'will rule them with an iron scepter and will dash them to pieces like pottery' —just as I have received authority from my Father. I will also give that one the morning star. Whoever has ears, let them hear what the Spirit says to the churches." Revelation 2:26-29

This passage begins, *"To the one who is victorious and does my will to the end..."*

Our world has become notorious for "doing what I want". The message has become that I can do whatever I want as long as I am not hurting anyone. But the problem is that my determination to go my own way, write my own rules, live my life according to my desires or passions hurts the most important Person in all of life, and that Person is Jesus.

There is only one set of rules that counts and that is the set of rules that God set down. He wrote them because He knew they were the way to live life. He gave them, not so much as a mandate but more as a love letter to draw us to Him. His Book, that we call the law, should be seen much more like being wrapped into a protective warm hug than a slap on the hand. It is Him telling us the way to make life work.

We cannot try to change His Word to make it fit us. He wants to change us to make us fit His Word.

Victory will be ours if we submit to His plan. But we need help. We have all broken His law, wrong thoughts, wrong actions, wrong words, wrong motives. We have all gone our own way. We need to come to the One who is THE WAY, ask for forgiveness, and submit to His plan.

"When I shut up the heavens so that there is no rain, or command locusts to devour the land or send a plague among my people, if my people, who are called by my name, will humble themselves and pray and seek my face and turn from their wicked ways, then I will hear from heaven, and I will forgive their sin and will heal their land." 2 Chronicles 7:13-14

We must ask. We must repent. He is listening. He is waiting to wrap us up in His protective embrace and bring victory into our lives.

REVELATION

CHAPTER 3

DAY 20

Years ago, our grandmother died. A friend of hers came into the funeral home. She told us she had never seen Grandma look more beautiful. I guess that funeral make-up was really good, because I always thought alive looked better than dead. Yet maybe sometimes make-up can almost make someone appear alive. Here's the thing, looking alive didn't change the fact that she was not.

That was the case with the church of Sardis. *"To the angel of the church in Sardis write: These are the words of him who holds the seven spirits of God and the seven stars. I know your deeds; you have a reputation of being alive, but you are dead." Revelation 3:1*

In this verse, Jesus addressed the church at Sardis. This city was located on a very high precipice. Because of their location, the city believed no enemies could get to them. It looked impenetrable. It wasn't. The enemies looked for areas that were vulnerable and unprotected. On several occasions, Sardis was invaded. It should have been a warning to them after it happened the first time, but according to history, it doesn't seem like they got it.

Sardis was a wealthy city, but the church at Sardis was really struggling spiritually. Jesus said, *"You have a reputation of being alive, but you are dead."* The Greek word here for dead is nekros. It's a word we use to describe a corpse. So, the people in this church looked like they were functioning. They looked like they were spiritually alive, but somehow, they had allowed themselves to be open to the enemy and the devil crept in, stealing their life. Just like the city had been invaded because of vulnerable, unprotected places, Satan found places in the spiritual lives of the people of Sardis that were vulnerable and unprotected.

Jesus challenged the people to examine their lives. Were they alive or dead? They needed to check their pulse. Maybe it's time for us to check our own pulse as well. Do we merely look like we're spiritually alive? Do we talk the talk, but on the inside, we're not growing and thriving? God wants us alive and growing today and every day. Yes, it's time to check our pulse.

Sardis needed a wake-up call and in the next couple of verses, that's what Jesus did with this church. Here's what it says: *"Wake up! Strengthen what remains and is about to die, for I have found your deeds unfinished in the sight of my God. Remember, therefore, what you have received and heard; hold it fast, and repent. But if you do not wake up, I will come like a thief, and you will not know at what time I will come to you."* Revelation 3:2-3

This church was dying spiritually. It told us in verse one that they only appeared to be alive. They looked like they were all okay, but they weren't. Again, this is a great challenge. How does the world see us? Do we put up a front that seems like we are followers of Christ?

This same message was the crux of Jesus' parable about the ten virgins. Five were ready and prepared. Five were not. Are we believers who are awake, prepared, functioning? Do we truly know Jesus? Do we love Him? Do we want to know Him better by studying His Word and praying?

Jesus also told the people of Sardis that their deeds were unfinished. What had they started but failed to complete?

How about us? Has God called us to do something? Did we start out obeying? But then maybe the cost seemed too high, or it was inconvenient to do, or we just would rather not, so we quit.

Jesus told the Sardis church that if they didn't wake up, He'd come like a thief. Yes, when the people would be completely caught off guard and unprepared, He said He would come. Paul also said that in *1 Thessalonians 5:1-3, "Now, brothers and sisters, about times and dates we do not need to write to you, for you know very well that the day of the*

Lord will come like a thief in the night. While people are saying, 'Peace and safety,' destruction will come on them suddenly, as labor pains on a pregnant woman, and they will not escape."

We must wake up, but how?

The Lord said to remember what we have received and heard, hold it fast, and repent.

Repentance is always the way back, because it means to turn and go the other direction, right back to the Lord.

Let's reflect over some situations from the Old Testament. When a whole lot of the world was going one way, God had a remnant that loved Him and followed Him. Sometimes it was merely a handful of people. That was the case with Noah and his family. While the whole world was doing its thing, Noah's family was doing God's thing. In the book of Daniel, Shadrach, Meshach, and Abednego refused to worship Nebuchadnezzar's statue. The three of them stood while the rest of Babylon bowed. It was pretty easy to see who was following the king's edict and who wasn't. It was three against everyone else. When Elijah challenged the prophets of Baal, it was 450 against 1.

Even during times of great corruption, God has always had people who love and follow Him. In the churches at Pergamum and Thyatira, there were a few bad among the good. In Sardis, there were a few good among the bad. But God did have a remnant. *"Yet you have a few people in Sardis who have not soiled their clothes. They will walk with me, dressed in white, for they are worthy. The one who is victorious will, like them, be dressed in white. I will never blot out the name of that person from the book of life, but will acknowledge that name before my Father and his angels. Whoever has ears, let them hear what the Spirit says to the churches." Revelation 3:4-6*

These verses tell us that it was just a few people who were dressed in white, a picture of being clothed in Christ's righteousness. When others were wallowing in the mire of sin, a few were following the Lord and His commandments, and their garments were not soiled. Most often, it is not the majority who love the Lord. Most often, it is merely a handful who will stand strong. But what a reward!

Jesus said for those who follow Him, He will never blot out their names from the Book of Life.

Again, let's do a little inventory. Are we a part of the majority or part of the remnant? Is our name indelibly written in the Book of Life?

It can be. It means asking Jesus to be our Lord and Savior. It begins with a prayer something like this:

Dear Jesus,

I know I am a sinner. I have gone my own way and have not followed You. Please forgive me for my sin and come into my life right now. I repent and receive You as my Savior and my Lord. Thank You for dying for me, shedding Your blood to wash away my sins. Please help me to live for You. Thank You, Lord, for saving me and making me Your child.

In Jesus' name,

Amen.

DAY 21

The book of Revelation is truly amazing. It only has twenty-two chapters, 404 verses, but includes references and allusions to hundreds of Old Testament Scriptures. We see one of those in this short passage. *"To the angel of the church in Philadelphia write: These are the words of him who is holy and true, who holds the key of David. What he opens no one can shut, and what he shuts no one can open. I know your deeds. See, I have placed before you an open door that no one can shut. I know that you have little strength, yet you have kept my word and have not denied my name." Revelation 3:7-8*

Isaiah 22 says that when God opens a door, it is opened, and when He closes it, it's shut. That is so encouraging. It doesn't make any difference what the world says. If God calls us to do something and He wants the door opened, circumstances can't stand in the way. People can't negate God's call. Governments cannot shut it down. Even viruses, pandemics, global challenges can't stop God's work.

Jesus addressed the church at Philadelphia and as we look at His words, He only had good things to say to this group. His eyes were ever on them, so He knew that they had little strength left. They were tired, weary in well-doing, and yet they kept His Word.

This is the church I want to be a part of. This church loves Jesus.

But it wasn't easy. Persecution, ridicule, being hated, being scorned, all were part of the church of Philadelphia. The true church is always going to face challenges. The devil hates God's people and is not going to stand idle, while the church flourishes. He's going to fight, drumming up resistance and hard times.

It happened to Jesus.

It happened to His disciples.

It happened to the early church.

It happened to the church at Philadelphia.

It has happened throughout church history.

And it is happening to the church around the world today and perhaps has happened to us.

Jesus told us in Luke that we would have trouble, so we shouldn't be surprised when we do. We may see lots of situations that grieve our hearts. How much more must they grieve His heart?

Jesus told the Philadelphian church that He would have the final say. *"I will make those who are of the synagogue of Satan, who claim to be Jews though they are not, but are liars—I will make them come and fall down at your feet and acknowledge that I have loved you. Since you have kept my command to endure patiently, I will also keep you from the hour of trial that is going to come on the whole world to test the inhabitants of the earth."* Revelation 3:9-10

Someday the people who follow Satan will acknowledge truth. They will realize they were wrong, dead wrong.

For true believers, these words of Jesus are so sweet, so soothing. He told those who love and follow Him that He would keep them from the hour of trial that would come on the whole world to test earth's inhabitants.

Again, we ask, how close are we to that hour? In Matthew 24, the disciples questioned Jesus about that time. The Lord explained that famine, wars, earthquakes would come, and they would come like birth pains.

With the birth of a child, labor usually begins with a few twinges. On the way to the hospital a woman might even think, "Oh this labor thing is pretty easy. The pains aren't that bad." But as labor progresses, she becomes aware that labor is called labor for a reason. It's hard work. As the birth nears, the pains are no longer easy. Extremely intense, excruciating pains come fast and furious without even seconds between. That's how labor works. Pretty easy at first but by the time of the birth, it's fast and furious.

For years our world has had twinges, and then harder pains. In the last couple of years, globally we've had pestilences, famines, pandemics, earthquakes, natural disasters, wars, and they've come with not even seconds in between.

Kinda makes you think, doesn't it?

DAY 22

Jesus told them, *"I am coming soon. Hold on to what you have, so that no one will take your crown." Revelation 3:11*

Jesus cautioned the church at Philadelphia to hold on and protect the crown that they had coming. We cannot know for sure which crown this verse is referencing, because there are five different crowns spoken of in Scripture. They are the crown of rejoicing, the imperishable crown, the crown of glory, the crown of life, and the crown of righteousness.

My suspicion is that what is mentioned here is the crown of righteousness. *2 Timothy 4:8, "Now there is in store for me the crown of righteousness, which the Lord, the righteous Judge, will award to me on that day—and not only to me, but also to all who have longed for his appearing."*

A crown will be given if we are looking forward to His coming. A crown for each of us if we long for the time that we can be with Him.

Again, pestilences, famines, pandemics, earthquakes, natural disasters, wars have happened in recent days, so maybe we've said a little more often, "Come, Lord Jesus." For believers, it's easy to want Jesus to come back. We long to be in His presence.

Then someday, when we get to heaven, what will we do with any crowns we receive?

We see in *Revelation 4:10-11* that the twenty-four elders lay crowns at Jesus' feet. *"...They lay their crowns before the throne and say: 'You are worthy, our Lord and God, to receive glory and honor and power, for you created all things, and by your will they were created and have their being.'"*

How glad we will be to have a crown to lay at His feet. We will be so grateful to have something to offer Him. It will be our privilege to place it before the Lord. We'll give any crowns to the One who deserves all the crowns, all the glory, all the praise.

After all, He wore a crown for us. It had huge thorns and caused the blood to run down His face as He carried our sin.

And then Jesus also told them, *"The one who is victorious I will make a pillar in the temple of my God. Never again will they leave it. I will write on them the name of my God and the name of the city of my God, the new Jerusalem, which is coming down out of heaven from my God; and I will also write on them my new name. Whoever has ears, let them hear what the Spirit says to the churches." Revelation 3:12-13*

The Lord told the church at Philadelphia that He would make them pillars.

What does that mean?

Does it mean they're just going to stay in one spot, maybe playing heavenly music? A cloud, a harp, forever strumming eons of time away? This is the view that some people have of heaven. How sad.

I Corinthians 2 lets us know that we can't begin to fathom what heaven will be like. Because no eye has seen, no ear has heard, no human mind has conceived the things God has prepared for those who love him.

Just a cloud and a harp for eternity? Not remotely.

We read a little about the beauty of the Garden of Eden in Genesis. That garden was a real place here on earth. It was designed for Adam and Eve, and what little we know sounds absolutely amazing. So, we can only imagine how much more beautiful the place is that God is preparing for us when we join Him in His heavenly realm.

When we get to Revelation 21, we're going to see that building materials for the New Jerusalem include emeralds, gold, rubies, amethysts, sapphires to name a few. Here we use cement and stone, but God uses jewels and precious metals. It will be the most glorious, most wonderful adventure as we experience what

He has created for us. Plus, He will be there in all His glory. It is truly unfathomable.

So why pillars? Being a pillar in a community or in society denotes someone who is respected. It is a picture of strength. Jesus was telling John that the persecuted believers from Philadelphia would have a forever place in heaven. They were strong and victorious. The word victorious here means being an overcomer. They stood when others fell. They faced trials and they overcame. So just like pillars stand strong, that's how those believers would be in heaven.

1 John 5:3-5 tells us how we too can be overcomers, *"In fact, this is love for God: to keep his commands. And his commands are not burdensome, for everyone born of God overcomes the world. This is the victory that has overcome the world, even our faith. Who is it that overcomes the world? Only the one who believes that Jesus is the Son of God."*

To be an overcomer means we put our faith and trust in Jesus, because He has overcome the world.

Today, I am asking the Lord to help me stand strong, to be an overcomer. This is my prayer, but it's not only for me, it's also for everyone in my family, all my loved ones, all of you reading this, and the church around the world. Right now, I am praying for all of us to be overcomers.

"Whoever has ears, let him hear…"

DAY 23

One of my daughters, her husband, and their two kids live close to Chicago. I don't. My son-in-law's dad lives about thirty minutes from me, and his dad is struggling a bit physically. Getting older is not for the faint of heart. My son-in-law feels like he both wants and needs to spend more time with his dad. I've told him, "My house is your house. Come and go as you please." He came in a couple of days ago. As he was leaving, he gave me something. It's a pound of Canadian coffee. Someone sent it to him, but none of them drink coffee so he asked if I would like it. Um, YES! I've never tried Canadian coffee, and, after all, it is coffee. So of course, I'd like it. Coffee is one of my favorite things. I don't just like it, I love it. I start my day with a cup…sometimes two. But if I allow it to sit too long and it cools to lukewarm, I cannot drink it.

As we look at Laodicea, we're going to see that the Lord doesn't like lukewarm either.

We've looked at the letters to the first six churches. This now brings us to the seventh and final letter. *"To the angel of the church in Laodicea write…" Revelation 3:14*

In the other six letters, Jesus had some good things to say to the churches. Yes, some of the six had challenges, but even with those, there was a remnant that was doing what pleased the Lord. That is not what we see with this church. Sadly, there are only negatives.

As we study this section, we need to remember that there are no coincidences in God's Word. Every number, every name, every word is there on purpose, for a purpose. There are no extraneous words; there is nothing missing. God's Word is perfect.

Let's begin by looking at what the name Laodicea means, because when we look at the name of this church, it is incredibly significant.

Laodicea means the people's rights.

Think about that for a minute.

We've mentioned that each of these churches represent not only an individual church but also a church age. If that's the case, and this church is the last one, then it must be representative of the church at the end of days. That means that sadly there are people who call themselves part of "the church" who are living with a "my rights" mentality.

Does that fit with what we see?

So often we hear these words, "It's my right to..." and then that sentence is filled in with a number of phrases.

The People's Rights was the name of this church.

But wait a minute, as Christians, when we come to Christ and yield our lives to Him, what does that do to OUR rights?

If we claim to belong to Jesus, then what He asks of us is to follow His Word. When it's all said and done, we are to be His servants, and our responsibility is to do what He wants, not what we believe is our right to do. We lay our lives down; we lay our rights down, and we take up His cross and follow Him.

Today, people's rights have become the rule of the land and sadly that has even infiltrated the church. The authority is no longer God's Word. This is a very scary place to be. When we become the ultimate authority over what we want, God is shoved out and we sit on the throne of our own lives deciding what are "my rights".

Church, we must wake up. We are living in the days of Laodicea, and the admonitions that come next for this group are foreboding.

As we've said, Jesus only had reprimands for this church. *"To the angel of the church in Laodicea write: These are the words of the Amen, the faithful and true witness, the ruler of God's creation. I know your deeds, that you are neither cold nor hot. I wish you were either one*

or the other! So, because you are lukewarm—neither hot nor cold—I am
about to spit you out of my mouth." Revelation 3:14-16

God was telling them to choose one side or the other. They were comfortable in their "lukewarmness", but it was sickening to the Lord.

Too often we don't want to get out of our comfort zone. Our "lukewarmness" is sickening to the Lord.

Laodicea was located about six miles from the city of Hierapolis which had healing hot springs. Another city, Colossae, was about ten miles away and got the cold mountain streams. Hot for healing at Hierapolis, cold for refreshment and revitalizing at Colossae, but Laodicea had to pipe in their water. When the water arrived, the sediment, calcium carbonate, made it undrinkable until it settled. The water had to sit idle for a while, so it was always lukewarm.

Laodicea understood the analogy of being lukewarm. When something is lukewarm, it's in-between. It's riding the fence, no real commitment to be one or the other. And what did God say He would do? Spit, spew, vomit, actually this implies projectile vomiting, all words that could describe the Lord's utter distaste for lukewarmness.

Why? Because there is something that flourishes when it's lukewarm. It's yeast. And Jesus likened yeast to sin.

He told us that we are to be the salt of the earth, and salt kills yeast. But if we've lost our saltiness, if we become lukewarm, sin grows.

If we are lukewarm, we need to change. The Lord wants strong passionate believers who will say, "It makes no difference what the world tells me, I am standing firm on God's Word."

DAY 24

We're going to begin this day with an account that Jesus told. It's found in *Luke 12:16-21*, *"The ground of a certain rich man yielded an abundant harvest. He thought to himself, 'What shall I do? I have no place to store my crops.' Then he said, 'This is what I'll do. I will tear down my barns and build bigger ones, and there I will store my surplus grain. And I'll say to myself, "You have plenty of grain laid up for many years. Take life easy; eat, drink and be merry."' But God said to him, 'You fool! This very night your life will be demanded from you. Then who will get what you have prepared for yourself?' This is how it will be with whoever stores up things for themselves but is not rich toward God."*

Jesus told this as a warning. What are we spending our energy on? Is it merely stuff? Is it solely a more successful position? Is it just a bigger salary? The rich man had all he could ever want as far as material things. He had it all, and yet, he had nothing. He spent his life accumulating worldly possessions.

When someone wealthy dies, the question is sometimes asked, "How much did that person leave?"

The answer? "All of it."

It's what we see with the rich man. He didn't take even one kernel of grain into eternity with him.

Here in the book of Revelation, Jesus gave the people of Laodicea another warning. *"You say, 'I am rich; I have acquired wealth and do not need a thing.' But you do not realize that you are wretched, pitiful, poor, blind and naked. I counsel you to buy from me gold refined in the fire, so you can become rich; and white clothes to wear, so you can cover your shameful nakedness; and salve to put on your eyes, so you can see." Revelation 3:17-18*

Laodicea was a wealthy city. It was a banking hub. They had sheep that produced a rich, black, gorgeous wool. It was prized throughout the region. They had a medical school that developed a salve for eyes, and people came there to be treated.

The people of Laodicea appeared to have it all, wealth, wool for clothing, a treatment for their eyes. But God told them what they truly needed, gold that's refined in the fire, white clothes to wear, salve for their eyes that came from Him.

It was a warning for the church. It's a warning for us. Jesus did not mince words. He spoke very tough to this group with a stern rebuke.

As I look back on the growing up years of my children, I remember many of the fun sweet things that happened. But I also remember some of the times they disobeyed or tried to challenge my authority. They sometimes wanted to do their own thing, go their own way. Because I love them and wanted them to grow up to become the people God wanted them to be, I did discipline them. It was hard for me to do sometimes. It hurt me to dole out punishment. But because I wanted the very best for them, I did it.

Funny thing though, I never disciplined a stranger's kids. I didn't go to the grocery store and see someone else's children challenging their parents and step in to punish them. It's not that I never saw children disobeying, I did. But I never doled out punishment to a stranger's children.

Why?

They weren't my kids. I didn't know them. I didn't even know their names. I didn't love them the way I love my children.

But because I love my kids, I want the very best for them.

If we love our children, we will not allow them to grow up thinking they can do anything they want or have anything they want. We rein them in. We put restrictions on them that help them to do what is right. We rebuke and discipline the ones we love.

That is exactly what Jesus does in our lives. *"Those whom I love I rebuke and discipline. So be earnest and repent." Revelation 3:19*

This verse is addressed to the church at Laodicea. They needed the rebuke and the discipline.

Now, not all hard things are discipline and rebukes from the Lord, but here He told the church, that because He loved them, He would punish their disobedience. His great love is what was behind the rebuke.

We also see this in *Hebrews 12:4-6, "In your struggle against sin, you have not yet resisted to the point of shedding your blood. And have you completely forgotten this word of encouragement that addresses you as a father addresses his son? It says, 'My son, do not make light of the Lord's discipline, and do not lose heart when he rebukes you, because the Lord disciplines the one he loves, and he chastens everyone he accepts as his son.'"*

God wants to use everything that happens in our lives to draw us closer to Him.

Jesus lovingly rebuked the church at Laodicea calling them to repentance.

And as we've said before, repentance is the way back.

DAY 25

This week I received a "Save the Date" card in the mail. It told me that a wedding is on the horizon for my great-niece. Weddings are such lovely occasions; a young man and a young woman stand before God and make a covenant to forsake all others.

In this great book of Revelation, we've already addressed a bit about the bridegroom and the bride, but right now, we're going to revisit that from a Jewish perspective.

In Bible times, if a young man wanted to get married, he would go to the house of the prospective bride and knock on the door.

She had a choice to make. If she opened the door, she was saying yes to a possible marriage proposal. If she didn't open the door, she was refusing the bridegroom.

The one inside the house had to be the one to open the door. The one standing outside wasn't going to barge in. He wasn't going to beat down the door. He went, he knocked, and then he waited. The knock on the door came and inside the house there was a big decision. Yes or no.

There was no in-between. The open door was saying yes, and the closed door was saying no.

This is what Jesus says, *"Here I am! I stand at the door and knock. If anyone hears my voice and opens the door, I will come in and eat with that person, and they with me." Revelation 3:20*

This is so beautiful. The Bridegroom comes and knocks. If we open the door, He enters.

In the picture of the marriage proposal, the bridegroom brought several things with him. One was a bride price. He also brought a gift. And then finally, he brought with him a skein of wine. The first two gifts were offered to the family, but the wine was poured for the potential bride.

He handed her a cup and by offering it he was saying, "I am willing to give my life FOR you."

If she accepted the cup and drank, she was saying, "I am willing to give my life TO you."

It is what Jesus was offering during the last supper on the night He was betrayed. It is what He offers to us. The bride price was about to be paid with Jesus' own blood, His very life. He was paying it for each one of us with His death on the cross.

To us today, He offers the cup. As He holds it out to each of us, He is saying that He is willing to give His life FOR us.

In turn, we either take the cup He offers, or we don't.

Will we open the door, invite Him in, and then tell Jesus that we are giving our life TO Him?

He stands at the door and knocks.

It's our choice. What will we do? And it is an individual choice.

But let's also remember that Jesus addressed this to a church. He was standing outside. He was knocking. His heart's desire was to come in.

Laodicea is the church that means the people's rights. When people's rights reign supreme, the people themselves decide what goes on. People believe it is their right to make decisions based on what they think or feel.

Laodicea looked like a church.

They called themselves a church.

But what kind of church was it?

It was a church with Jesus on the outside.

This is one of the saddest things that can be said. The Lord Himself was outside which means the inside was merely a structure, an organization.

For Jesus to be on the inside, His entire Word must be taken for what it says, not merely what people decide might fit with what they want.

The book of John clarifies the identity of the Word in *John 1:1, "In the beginning was the Word, and the Word was with God, and the Word was God."* And then in *John 1:14, "The Word became flesh and made his dwelling among us. We have seen his glory, the glory of the one and only Son, who came from the Father, full of grace and truth."*

The bottom line is that Jesus is the Word, and the Word is Jesus. We cannot make a separation. Just because we may not like a portion of what the Bible says doesn't mean we can cast it aside. We don't get to vote on it. We don't get to decide that there are portions that are lovely and true and others that we deem archaic or not socially acceptable.

We don't get to pick and choose which parts we want and which ones we don't.

It's all or nothing.

To be the church of Jesus Christ is to put aside any rights we may think we have, follow Jesus with our whole hearts, and embrace every Word the Bible says.

DAY 26

I taught in a very small school in Southern Indiana for twenty-five years. One year the basketball team made it past sectionals. It was so exciting. Then came regionals. They walked out the victors that year and that had never happened. The dream of a lifetime became a reality for those boys to head to semi-state. I went to that game and as I looked around, I was convinced almost every person from that very small town was there to cheer on the team. I knew all the boys playing. I had most in my classes and the ones I didn't, I still knew because at that school almost everyone knew everyone. It was such a thrill, but it got even bigger. They won semi-state. On to the final game. I couldn't attend that one in person, but I was glued to the TV. Every play, every basket brought that little school closer to what at one time seemed completely out of reach, and when the final buzzer sounded, my school won.

What does it mean to be victorious?

In sports, it may mean climbing a ladder and cutting down the net. I know on that day for my little school's team, cutting down that net did imply victory. The final score made it clear my school's team was the winner.

In other situations, being victorious may mean a special ring or a trophy of some type. In the political realm, it means the one who received the most votes. In battle, it is watching the foe you've defeated turn around and retreat.

It is glorious to be on the winning side.

From a spiritual perspective, what does it mean to be victorious? We've already talked about the fact that being victorious means being an overcomer. We see that in 1 John 5.

But being victorious also means we have chosen the winning side. That is to follow Jesus. The entire Bible is about the Messiah. Over and over again there are passages that point us to Him. From Genesis to Revelation and every book in between, we can see Jesus on every page. As we study the book of Revelation, we are going to unveil the final battle. When we read the end of the Book, we see that no matter how hard the devil fights, no matter what he tries to do, Jesus is the victor.

If we want to end up on the winning side, we must follow the Savior. And then this is what happens for those of us who do. *"To the one who is victorious, I will give the right to sit with me on my throne, just as I was victorious and sat down with my Father on his throne. Whoever has ears, let them hear what the Spirit says to the churches."* Revelation 3:21-22

Someday, we will have the amazing privilege of joining the King of Kings on His throne. Romans 8:17 tells us that as followers of the Lord Jesus we become joint heirs with Him. Joint heirs! It's why He gives us the ability to sit on the throne with Him. How amazing that we get to join Him as He rules and reigns!

What does it really mean to be victorious?

Know Christ as your Savior and Lord.

REVELATION
CHAPTER 4

DAY 27

As we have already said, there are many who believe Revelation 1:19 is an outline for the entire book. John was told to write what he had seen, what was happening then, and what would take place later. In other words, write what was, what is, and what is to come.

Remember, some scholars have called this verse the divine outline. Now, let me qualify this with the fact that there are those who don't agree, but we are writing this, and we have to write it the way we see it. If someday we are proved wrong because there is a different timing to the events in this book, that's okay. No one has this prophecy thing down pat. We walk in the light we have. Misunderstanding the timing of events doesn't change the events, it only changes our understanding of the time.

John was told to write the things that he had seen, write what was happening then, and finally what would take place later. In the Greek, the phrase that describes what would happen later is meta tauta.

Verse 1 of chapter 4 begins with that phrase, meta tauta, and it means, after this. So, the question we ask is, after what? And for some scholars the answer is, after the church age, and again, we are in that camp. We believe the next major event on the horizon for the church is the rapture.

Keep in mind, the rapture is not the same as the second coming. The second coming happens when Jesus comes to earth to plant His feet on the Mount of Olives. We see that in Zechariah 14, Acts 1, and Revelation 19. Everyone on earth will see this happen and it occurs at the end of the seven-year time period known as the tribulation.

The rapture is when Jesus comes unexpectedly to snatch the church, His bride, out of this world, up to heaven, and to the Marriage Supper of the Lamb. The word used in the Bible is harpazó, which means a catching away or snatching away. The word rapture, used to describe the event, is taken from Latin. It is derived from rapio which means to be caught up or snatched away. Just think how marvelous it will be when Jesus comes to catch His bride, the church, up in His arms and carry us over the threshold into our new life that begins with the Marriage Supper of the Lamb.

To be honest, this is a debated subject in church circles. Not everyone agrees on the timing. And that is perfectly fine. Our counsel is to study the Scripture, so we each know what we believe. There is coming a day when we will all agree because this event will have taken place and we will know the exact truth, the perfect timing. It will be completely understood after it takes place. We see through a glass darkly, so our job is to read the Bible, study, look at the signs, know their meaning, wake up to what is going on.

The Bible is this beautiful book that fits together like pieces of a puzzle. The Old Testament points forward. The New Testament points forward, but also backward, and every word in the Scripture is for us today. The Word of God is what was, what is, and what is to come. The events, the lives of the people in the Scripture are real moments in history, but they were also shadows of things that would take place later. It is one of the evidences that God is the author of this book.

DAY 28

Today, let's look at some of the shadows, the hints in the Scripture pointing forward to what the rapture might look like.

Genesis 5:21 tells us about a man named Enoch. He was sixty-five when he became the father of Methuselah. The Scripture says he walked faithfully with God, and he did it for 300 years. Don't you just long for that to be true of us, that we walk faithfully with God? Now, we probably won't live another 300 years, but we can make every day we do have count. And then, verse 24, *"Enoch walked faithfully with God; then he was no more, because God took him away."*

God came and caught Enoch up in His arms and carried him away. That brings tears to my eyes. No fuss, no muss, no sticky business of having to die. One moment he was here and then suddenly he was there. One minute he was looking at terra firma and the next he was gazing into the eyes of the One he had served faithfully for all those years.

That same thing is on the church's agenda. It is going to happen one of these days.

1 Thessalonians 4:13-18 and 5:1-11 talk about this as do other passages. I believe that this is the next big, and when I say big, I mean ginormous, event on the church calendar. Can you imagine how glorious it will be when in that one moment we are here, and the next we are gazing into the eyes of our Bridegroom? And we believe it could happen any second now.

And to that we say, "Amen. Come, Lord Jesus."

2 Kings 2 gives us another shadow of this event. A prophet named Elijah, one named Elisha, and some other prophets of God, knew an incredible secret. A rapture was imminent. God was coming to take His servant Elijah up to heaven. Elijah served God faithfully. He stood against the evil King Ahab and his wicked queen, Jezebel. He took on the prophets of Baal. Elijah told Ahab it wouldn't rain for several years, and Ahab hated him and made his life miserable because of it. Elijah's life was not easy. Believe me, he wasn't popular with the reigning authorities. His life was threatened. He had a bounty on his head. There was a cost for this man to follow God.

And yet, he served God. He faithfully trusted and obeyed the Lord. But then the day came when his job was done; it was time to come home. It was time for a rest. So, the Lord sent a chariot to pick him up, and this wasn't any old run-of-the-mill chariot that you could purchase at the local chariot shop, either. It came right out of heaven, blazing with fire, even the horses were on fire. This was worlds bigger than a Hollywood movie. Then, the whole thing ascended to heaven in a whirlwind. Elijah was here and then in a flash, he was there.

Okay, can you see why rapture is an appropriate word for this event? The magnificent joy, the pure ecstasy, the overwhelming delight and bliss and euphoria for Elijah…we can't even begin to imagine.

This same kind of event is on the horizon for the bride of Christ. Enoch was snatched up. Elijah was taken up. And then here in *Revelation 4:1* we see another hint of a rapture because John was called up, *"Come up here, and I will show you what must take place after this."*

And instantly he was in the presence of the Lord.

One of these days, the church, the bride of Christ will be gloriously caught up in the arms of the Savior. We will meet our Bridegroom face-to-face, and we will be carried away to our new life.

RAPTURE!

"After this I looked, and there before me was a door standing open in heaven. And the voice I had first heard speaking to me like a trumpet said, 'Come up here, and I will show you what must take place after this.'"
Revelation 4:1

What John saw before him was an open door. Right now, the door is standing wide open. Anyone who wishes can enter.

In Luke 14, Jesus told a parable about a great banquet. The invitations went out. Then as a gentle reminder, a servant was sent to call those who were invited, to come. The banquet was ready. But the answers to the invitation came in the form of excuses. One had purchased a field, one had some new oxen, another had just gotten married. Too busy, too tied up, too caught up in the things of the world to say yes.

The invitation wasn't for work. It wasn't washing windows. It wasn't a boring conference. It wasn't an invitation for some trial medical procedure. It was a banquet. It was feasting and fellowship and celebrating and wonderful food and great rejoicing and pampering and deliciousness and...

It was a banquet.

Why wouldn't someone come to a banquet? But for the sake of a bit of land, a few cows, a relationship, they missed it. They chose the ordinary and missed the exquisite.

Right now, the door is standing open. The invitation is going out. We are invited to the banquet that lasts for eternity. There is feasting and fellowship and awesomeness and joy and celebrating and Jesus the Bridegroom and God Almighty and heaven and family and friends and...

It's a banquet. Are we making excuses for why we won't come? Are we missing the eternal for the sake of the temporal?

IT'S A BANQUET!

The door is still open. Don't miss it.

DAY 29

"*At once I was in the Spirit, and there before me was a throne in heaven with someone sitting on it. And the one who sat there had the appearance of jasper and ruby. A rainbow that shone like an emerald encircled the throne. Surrounding the throne were twenty-four other thrones, and seated on them were twenty-four elders. They were dressed in white and had crowns of gold on their heads. From the throne came flashes of lightning, rumblings and peals of thunder. In front of the throne, seven lamps were blazing. These are the seven spirits of God. Also in front of the throne there was what looked like a sea of glass, clear as crystal.*" Revelation 4:2-6

Can you see it?

Right here in chapter 4 of the Revelation, a veil is lifted for us to see the exquisite beauty of the Lord.

I have seen some beautiful places in the world. The snowcapped mountains in Colorado, the forests of Yellowstone, the view from the edge of the Grand Canyon, the oceans, the star- studded skies, there have been moments that I have been reduced to silent awe. These places have resulted in praise and honor pouring out of me, sometimes in laughter, sometimes in tears. They have also brought moments when I can scarcely breathe because of the beauty and majesty.

And that has happened just looking at this wonderful creation.

But a new sight awaits us. There is coming a day when we will get our first glimpse of the Lord. We will see the One who, with a Word, created all this beauty. We will see the One we call Almighty God, Savior, and Friend. We will no longer see through the glass darkly, but rather face-to-face. It may take us awhile to lift our faces off the ground, but we will have all of eternity to do it.

John gives us a brief description of what he was privileged to view. He saw ruby and jasper and emerald and rainbow. He saw flashes of lightning and heard rumblings and peals of thunder. He saw what looked like a sea of glass. He saw the Lord God who was seated on the throne in heaven.

What a sight! No place on earth even comes close.

"In the center, around the throne, were four living creatures, and they were covered with eyes, in front and in back. The first living creature was like a lion, the second was like an ox, the third had a face like a man, the fourth was like a flying eagle. Each of the four living creatures had six wings and was covered with eyes all around, even under its wings. Day and night they never stop saying: 'Holy, Holy, Holy is the Lord God Almighty, who was, and is, and is to come.'" Revelation 4:6-8

Around the throne of God in heaven were four living creatures. From this passage they appear rather frightening, a lion, an ox, a man, a flying eagle.

Who are they?

Alright, here is one of those treasure hunts. We must go all the way back to the tabernacle in the book of Exodus. We read about the Israelites camping around the tabernacle, the place of God's presence. In Numbers 2 it tells us that there was an order for how they placed their tents, three of the Israelite tribes to the east, three to the north, three to the west, and finally three to the south. And they had banners under which they camped. To the east toward the sunrise, three tribes camped under the banner for Judah, and it was a lion. To the north was the standard for Dan, an eagle, west was Ephraim, the ox, and south was Reuben, and that banner was a man. Around the tabernacle were the lion, the eagle, the ox, and the man. Interesting, isn't it?

In the book of Ezekiel, chapter 1, Ezekiel sees similar creatures. And again, the lion, the eagle, the ox, and a man, Ezekiel 10 tells us they are cherubim.

Now, have you ever seen a picture of baby angels with little wings, and they are called cherubim? That is not what cherubim look like. They are awesome, big, impressive beings. We would be awestruck in their presence.

And then we move into the New Testament with the four Gospels. As we study, we see that each reveals a facet of Jesus' character. In Matthew, the focus is Jesus as King, the Lion of Judah. In Mark, we see Him as the suffering Servant, the ox or bull ready to be sacrificed. In Luke, He is described as the Son of Man. And in John, He is the Lord our God, represented by the flying eagle.

Then here in Revelation 4, we see these four living creatures surrounding the throne. The Scripture says they are like the lion, the ox, the man, and the eagle. And their job is to give praise and glory and honor to the Lord who is King of Kings, the Perfect Sacrifice, the Son of Man, and God Almighty.

Perhaps the reason these creatures look like this is because they reflect His glory as they spend all their time in God's presence.

Perhaps a big part of our job is to start to look like Him and reflect His glory as we spend time in His presence.

In Revelation 4 and 5, we read about heaven. The question is, how do we get there? How can we know that we will be in heaven?

The answer is simple enough for a child but profound enough to challenge the minds of the world's greatest thinkers.

People call it the Good News.

Let's go to the book of Romans.

Romans 3:23 tells us that we are all sinners.

Romans 6:23 explains that the wages for our sin is death. So far this doesn't sound like good news but rather bad news.

But the verse doesn't stop there. It goes on to say that the gift of God is eternal life through Jesus Christ. Did you see that? There is a gift.

What do we do with a gift?

We receive it. We receive the gift of eternal life by repenting and asking the Lord for salvation.

Romans 10:13 says that everyone who calls on the name of the Lord will be saved.

Now that is very Good News!

It takes a moment to receive this gift, but it takes a lifetime to live it out.

We have a clue in the next few verses how to begin that.

"Whenever the living creatures give glory, honor and thanks to him who sits on the throne and who lives for ever and ever, the twenty-four elders fall down before him who sits on the throne and worship him who lives for ever and ever. They lay their crowns before the throne and say: 'You are worthy, our Lord and God, to receive glory and honor and power, for you created all things, and by your will they were created and have their being.'" Revelation 4:9-11

This begins with worship.

I want to clear up something that might be a stumbling block for people. Some people portray heaven as boring, sitting, yawning while quietly strumming a harp. And others portray hell as the happening party place where you indulge all your senses. Neither is correct.

Heaven is a place that is so magnificent, so incredibly stunning, that our hearts will soar and nearly explode out of the sheer joy of being there. Words will fail, laughter will bubble forth, tears will roll down our cheeks, our souls will sing, our breath will catch. Why? Because it's what we were created for. We are beings who are created to worship. We are created for worship and praise to burst out of us. It is the very thing for which we were made. And so, in heaven we will have opportunity after opportunity to experience the sheer magnificent pleasure of worshiping, not the creation, but the Creator.

These few verses show worship around the throne, but heaven won't be the place where that is all we do. Because everything we do there will be an act of worshiping the One who made it possible. When we indulge in eating the most delectable food, when we fellowship with family and friends, when we walk hand in hand with Jesus, when we run and jump and play like we did as children, when we sing at the top of our lungs and it actually sounds great, when we sit down to have lunch with Moses or Daniel or John, when we learn the secrets of the universe and it makes sense to us, when we...

Heaven will not, not even for one nanosecond of all eternity, be boring, sitting, and yawning away our time. It will be the place for which we were created, and for which we fit perfectly, and for which we will thrive and flourish and experience true peace, shalom, joy because it will be home.

Hell, on the other hand, is the place for which we were not created to be. Stay tuned for our teaching on what hell will be like.

REVELATION

CHAPTER 5

DAY 30

Revelation 5 begins, *"Then I saw..." Revelation 5:1*

Three simple words, but there is a great challenge in these few words for us. *"Then I saw..."* What do we see? What do we see when we open the Word and read? Do we pay attention? Do we apply what we read? Do we glance but not really see because we're too busy or too preoccupied?

John looked with eyes that could see because He trusted the One who was revealing it all to him. He was looking. He was noticing. He was taking in everything all around him. Moment by moment, as the vision was unfolding, he was recording what he saw. He wrote it down for all generations to see.

Yes, he was experiencing it, but we have the privilege of holding all of it in our hands. It is complete for us from beginning to end. We also have the advantage of using it as the tool to measure what is going on in our world. We get to place the book of Revelation right next to our news feed and plot the events on a timeline to assess where we are.

There are two sides to this coin.

Looking at the condition of the world...disease, tornadoes, earthquakes in various places, floods, the economy, government control, truth being thrown to the ground, fires... we need to have eyes to see.

Looking at the condition of the world...the hand of God, people repenting, the Gospel being preached throughout the airwaves, churches coming together, loving people...we need to have eyes to see.

What was it John saw?

"Then I saw in the right hand of him who sat on the throne a scroll with writing on both sides and sealed with seven seals." Revelation 5:1

He saw a scroll, and this scroll was in the right hand of the One who was seated on the throne. The right hand means power. It means strength. It means rule and order, even when it looks to the world like everything is falling apart.

It means the Lord has it under control. God knows and sees everything facing our world. Nothing has caught Him by surprise. Nothing is out of His control even when it seems to us to be spinning out of our control.

This scroll had writing on both sides. Normally a scroll would be written on one side and then rolled up and sealed. This one had no more place for writing. It was completely covered. The message from this scroll could not be added to or changed. What had been written, had been written, and it will happen. There is no changing it.

It was sealed with seven seals. Throughout this book of Revelation, the number seven appears frequently. It is the number of completeness. What has been written on this scroll is what we need to know.

It was in His right hand. It was complete. He knows the beginning and He knows the end and every moment in between. It is a message we can rely on and trust.

DAY 31

"*And I saw a mighty angel proclaiming in a loud voice, 'Who is worthy to break the seals and open the scroll?' But no one in heaven or on earth or under the earth could open the scroll or even look inside it. I wept and wept because no one was found who was worthy to open the scroll or look inside.*" *Revelation 5:2-4*

This passage is filled with such despair. The message was right there. John wanted to know what it said, and yet he saw no one who could open it.

What if we approached reading and studying God's message to us with the same eagerness and desire that John approached this scroll? What if we felt despair if we could not open the Bible or hear someone read from it? How would the Lord reward that kind of passion and fervor? What would we glean from Jesus' Words to us if we approached it as if nothing else in all of creation mattered as much as hearing it?

When have we been brokenhearted because we couldn't hear a message or have Bible study or sing praises?

What would happen within the church if our passion became so great for the Word that it would bring us to tears if we couldn't hear?

John wept uncontrollably because no one was found who was worthy to open the scroll. There wasn't a single person throughout all time, among all humanity, who was worthy. It all appeared hopeless.

But then, the message came that there was One who was able.

"Then one of the elders said to me, 'Do not weep! See, the Lion of the tribe of Judah, the Root of David, has triumphed. He is able to open the scroll and its seven seals.'" Revelation 5:5

The message could be opened. It could be read, but only because the Lion of the tribe of Judah was qualified to open it. And He is qualified.

Jesus came as the Lamb of God, the perfect sacrifice. He laid down His life, shedding His blood to wash away our sins. His death looked to the world as if He had been defeated, but He conquered the very death that put Him in the grave. He triumphed and brought the victory out of the grave with Him, so we will triumph too.

He is the only One who was qualified to open the scroll. And He did. The message of the world's last events that will take place was outlined in this scroll. He revealed all we need to know.

No matter what things look like, do not weep.

The Lion of the tribe of Judah has triumphed.

DAY 32

What was the extent of the torture and abuse that our Savior suffered? We have seen movies attempting to portray it, but I believe it is only a glimpse. He was carrying every bit of guilt and shame for every sin, for every person. Dr. Luke does tell us He sweat drops of blood in the Garden of Gethsemane. This very rare medical condition is caused by extreme emotional stress. It results in weakness and possible shock.

After His arrest, He became the sport of the moment by being blindfolded, struck, His beard pulled out, whipped, flogged, tormented, spat upon. Battered, blood loss, dehydration, bruised, the Scripture in Isaiah tells us He no longer resembled a man. Forced to carry the weight of the heavy cross on top of the entire weight of the sin of the world, most likely stripped naked, crucified with nails through His hands and feet, hours of torture trying to breathe, finally inhaling for the last time, He died in total agony.

The slain Lamb of God...

"Then I saw a Lamb, looking as if it had been slain, standing at the center of the throne, encircled by the four living creatures and the elders. The Lamb had seven horns and seven eyes, which are the seven spirits of God sent out into all the earth." Revelation 5:6

And why did He do it? Because of a love that is bigger, more far reaching, all-encompassing, a love that wanted mankind to come into a relationship with Him. The sin had to be washed away. The only blood that could make sinful man clean was the perfect blood of the perfect Lamb. Seven horns, His complete power. Seven eyes, He sees all. The seven spirits of God, His absolute completeness.

He is omnipotent.

He is omniscient.

He is omnipresent.

The perfect One offered His perfect life in His horrific death.

John saw a Lamb looking as if it had been slain. The power that brought us life is the crucified Lamb of God because His death brought life to us.

And Jesus had the right. He had the purpose. He had the willing heart to take the scroll.

"He went and took the scroll from the right hand of him who sat on the throne. And when he had taken it, the four living creatures and the twenty-four elders fell down before the Lamb. Each one had a harp and they were holding golden bowls full of incense, which are the prayers of God's people." Revelation 5:7-8

What a glorious moment this must have been. John saw this One who had been slain, was dead, but is now alive forever. Jesus took the scroll and immediately worship began. This act of getting ready to open the scroll was so momentous that the four living creatures and all the twenty-four elders fell before Him.

They had harps, which are instruments of praise.

They had golden bowls filled with incense, which is a perfumed substance made up of costly sweet-smelling spices that was used for worship. But this incense is even more costly and sweet because it was made from the prayers of God's people.

What does that say to us? Our prayers can be filled with joy and wonder. They can be filled with tears and requests. They can be for those nearest to us or those around the world. Our prayers can be sung or shouted or whispered or silent. We can pray any time, any place, any season. We don't need a title or position or education or talent or wardrobe or credentials to pray. He hears all our prayers as His children, and they are a sweet perfume to our Savior. He loves it when we pray.

Why not pray right now?

DAY 33

A nd then the worship music began.

"And they sang a new song, saying: 'You are worthy to take the scroll and to open its seals, because you were slain, and with your blood you purchased for God persons from every tribe and language and people and nation. You have made them to be a kingdom and priests to serve our God, and they will reign on the earth.'" Revelation 5:9-10

They sang a new song. Maybe we need to read that again. They sang a new song.

I can't tell you how many times I've heard complaints about music within the church. They range from style, to melody, to repetition, to decibels, to beat, to one or two words. I'm not sure there has been a time in church history when people haven't fought over music. Much of the time the cry is to go back to the old music.

These verses today challenge that mindset. It is actually a command that we see issued here to sing a new song to the Lord.

I guess the question is why.

I don't think we will know this side of heaven the complete answer to that question, but let me share a few reasons that I suspect.

Jesus Christ is so incredible that there are not enough songs to be written that could cover all of what He has done and who He is.

The wide range of music reaches the wide range of people who need to hear the messages of the songs.

Each of us is touched at different times by the music. I might not need a song of comfort today but could well need one tomorrow.

Music is personal to me, but it is also personal to the Lord.

Even the same words set to different tunes strike different chords in our hearts.

Music flows like a river. It cannot be stopped.

People from every nation, tribe, language, people group have unique ways of expressing prayers and praise to Him. Genuine worship is always worthy of being sung.

There are lovely songs written by those who have suffered little but have walked paths of joy and celebration with the Lord. There are lovely songs written by those who have suffered much and faced persecution for the Lord. There are lovely songs written by those new to the faith. There are lovely songs written by those who have lived the faith for years.

Songs written by those who see

Songs written by those who are blind

Songs written by those who can hear

Songs written by those who cannot

Songs written by those who are ill

Songs written by those who are well

Songs written in times of loss

Songs written in times of plenty

"And they sang a new song."

DAY 34

We walk into our churches as the worship begins.

Wrong!

The worship began eons ago. It has been happening in the heavens for millennia. We never begin worship, rather we join worship. Thousands, no ten thousand times ten thousand, are worshiping at this very moment.

"Then I looked and heard the voice of many angels, numbering thousands upon thousands, and ten thousand times ten thousand. They encircled the throne and the living creatures and the elders." Revelation 5:11

What does that sound like? What complete joy and thrill will there be when we have the opportunity to look and hear all of those voices raised in praise to the One who sits on the throne? When we get the first glimpse of the One who shed His blood that we might live with Him forever, how great will our thanksgiving be that He loves us that much?

Talk about a worship service. Every voice will bring beauty; every voice will raise praise; every voice will add to the chorus.

What a day that will be!

What a contrast we have from this passage and the moments when Jesus Christ, the Lamb of God, was crucified. He was mocked, spit on, abused, beaten, made fun of, and crucified by the people surrounding Him.

But heaven sees who He really is.

"In a loud voice they were saying: 'Worthy is the Lamb, who was slain, to receive power and wealth and wisdom and strength and honor and glory and praise!'" Revelation 5:12

The line drawn in the sand raises the question: "Who do we believe He is?" If we believe Him to be an ordinary man, cut down in His prime after teaching some good lessons, merely a man like one of us, then we miss everything about Him.

If we understand that He is Immanuel, God with us, who became the sacrifice and took away the sin of the world, conquered death, is alive, and waiting for an invitation to come into our lives, then we gain everything.

"Then I heard every creature in heaven and on earth and under the earth and on the sea, and all that is in them, saying: 'To him who sits on the throne and to the Lamb be praise and honor and glory and power, for ever and ever!'" Revelation 5:13

Can you imagine? Every voice with one unified message bringing praise, honor, glory, and power forever!

What a moment that will be. Nothing we have ever known will compare. It will be with such gratitude and love that we will join this chorus.

We can hardly wait!

And this chorus then ends with this one word, "Amen".

The word amen is one of the best-known words in all human speech. I think it is because it is a very similar word in many different languages. It can mean truly or may it be so.

These living creatures are declaring the truth of everything that is being said. And right after their declaration they fall down and worship.

"The four living creatures said, 'Amen,' and the elders fell down and worshiped." Revelation 5:14

Today we want to echo those voices in heaven, "Amen" and fall down and worship.

REVELATION
CHAPTER 6

DAY 35

Once again, we come to the number seven. We already addressed how frequently we see this number in Scripture, but Revelation is filled with sevens.

In chapter 6 we begin with the opening of seven seals. *"I watched as the Lamb opened the first of the seven seals." Revelation 6:1*

Let's remember that the Bible is 66 different books, scribed by 40+ authors, over 1500 years. These writers came from all different walks of life: kings, servants, priests, shepherds, prophets, prisoners, some rich, some poor. And they were all led by the Holy Spirit as to what to write. Many authors and yet throughout the Bible we see this same pattern of sevens.

Here are just a few…

Seven days of creation

Noah went into the ark and seven days later the rain came

Seven clean animals

Seven holy days in Leviticus 23

A seven-branched lampstand in the tabernacle and later in the Temple

Joshua and the Israelites marched around Jericho seven days and then seven times on the seventh day

Seventy years of the Babylonian captivity

Naaman was told to wash in the Jordan River seven times

Seven deacons were chosen in the book of Acts

And there are many more.

This is referred to as the heptadic structure, and we see it repeatedly both overtly and hidden within the Hebrew and Greek texts. It is one of the fingerprints of God on His Word.

This pattern of sevens begins within the Hebrew text of Genesis 1:1. Let's dig into that. In our English translation, it is ten words. *"In the beginning God created the heavens and the earth."*

But in Hebrew the first verse of Genesis 1 is actually seven words.

It looks like this: בְּרֵאשִׁית בָּרָא אֱלֹהִים אֵת הַשָּׁמַיִם וְאֵת הָאָרֶץ׃

I love that this is how our Bible begins.

Now, let's look at one more thing in the Hebrew text of Genesis 1:1. Do you notice the word right in the middle of the verse? It's only two letters: אֵת

I find this amazing, because this word doesn't translate into a spoken word. It's placed there but not read. So, what are these two letters? If they're not read, why are they there?

They are the aleph and the tav. They are the first letter of the Hebrew alphabet and the last.

In the Greek language, we would recognize the first and last letters as the alpha and the omega.

Yes, this is the Alpha and the Omega.

That's what we see right smack in the middle of verse one of the Bible…the First and the Last. In Revelation 1:17, Jesus says, "I am the First and the Last."

Coincidence? Not a chance!

DAY 36

Okay now, we want to give you a heads-up. As we open the pages to Revelation 6, we are going to see some verses that are challenging. You've probably heard of the four horsemen of the Apocalypse. This is where they are introduced. It's a little like being in the middle of a mystery as we see this Revelation unfold piece by piece. We're going to take this one step at a time. God has it all in His control. Remember, these pieces do come together, and He wins!

Here in Revelation 6, the first of the seven seals is opened. Years ago, important documents were written on scrolls and then sealed with wax until the time was right for the document to be opened.

Let's look at seal one. Up to this point, John saw some things taking place in heaven. What he saw, beginning in this chapter, is what will be taking place here on earth.

"I watched as the Lamb opened the first of the seven seals. Then I heard one of the four living creatures say in a voice like thunder, 'Come!' I looked, and there before me was a white horse! Its rider held a bow, and he was given a crown, and he rode out as a conqueror bent on conquest." Revelation 6:1-2

As we look at these verses, let's be reminded of who the Lamb is. In chapter 5 the Lamb was revealed. This is Jesus, the One who was slain, the One who shed His blood to purchase our salvation. The Lamb is the One opening the seals.

As the first seal is opened, we see the rider of a white horse who is being summoned by the thunderous command, "Come!"

Who is this on a white horse?

The rider is one who appears to be a conquering hero. Some have thought that perhaps this is Jesus, because in Revelation 19, we do see Jesus coming on a white horse.

But this rider is not the Lord. In these verses, the one on the horse is trying to look like the Messiah. He is deceiving the world with his appearance. He carries a bow. There are a couple of different ways scholars have looked at this. It can indicate a weapon, his willingness to fight. But if you notice, there are no arrows. He appears to come in peace. But it could also mean he carries a sign of covenant, just like God gave Noah a rainbow in the sky. My thinking is that it most likely indicates both. This rider makes treaties, agreements, promises, but he is bent on conquest. The world acknowledges him as a global leader. He is given a crown.

Throughout history, Satan's goal has been to emulate God. He has wanted worship and to become the ultimate ruler.

The rider of this white horse is the antichrist.

What are some characteristics of this evil one?

In 2 Thessalonians 2, he is referred to as a man of lawlessness, one who will exalt himself over everything that is called God and will proclaim himself to be God.

We find him referenced in *Daniel 11:36, "The king will do as he pleases. He will exalt and magnify himself above every god and will say unheard-of things against the God of gods. He will be successful until the time of wrath is completed, for what has been determined must take place."*

But let's not be confused. He may think he comes to rule. He may believe he has the power to overthrow God. But he will be subject to God's will. In this passage from Revelation, when he is commanded to "Come", he must.

And so, with the opening of the first seal, we have the appearance of the antichrist on the stage of end time events. This then is the tribulation period.

Back in March of 2020, Pope Francis added his voice to a call for a worldwide ceasefire so people could focus on dealing with the coronavirus. Literally, what he was asking for was global peace.

At the writing of this devotion from Revelation, world peace has not yet happened. But what event, or series of events, will take place that will cause the world to clamor for a time of apparent peace?

And then also during the pandemic and since, the word safety has been heard over and over.

"For your safety, stay in."

"We are doing this to keep you safe."

People sometimes end messages on TV, texts, social media, or phone calls with this phrase, "Stay safe".

This was completely unprecedented, like nothing we had ever seen. And under the guise of safety, things changed drastically. It's kind of amazing how fast the world gravitated toward what governments mandated under the pretext of being safe.

Peace and safety were espoused on a global level. It was a good taste of things yet on the horizon. During the end times, the man of lawlessness will appear to bring peace. One of the names for Jesus is Prince of Peace. But the man of sin, that one who will appear to be a messiah, will attempt to emulate the TRUE Messiah and at first try to usher in peace. But this will be a false sense of peace and it will not last.

Daniel 8:25, "He will cause deceit to prosper, and he will consider himself superior. When they feel secure, he will destroy many and take his stand against the Prince of princes. Yet he will be destroyed, but not by human power."

1 Thessalonians 5:3 states, "While people are saying, 'Peace and safety,' destruction will come on them suddenly, as labor pains on a pregnant woman, and they will not escape."

Destruction will come when people are lulled into a false sense of peace and safety.

Peace will not be long lasting. We see that with the opening of the second seal and the entrance of the next rider, *"When the Lamb opened the second seal, I heard the second living creature say, 'Come!' Then another horse came out, a fiery red one. Its rider was given power to take peace from the earth and to make people kill each other. To him was given a large sword." Revelation 6:3-4*

War, murder, and annihilation are going to be part of the end times. This is the second seal.

This is challenging. People's hearts long for peace. We want to know that our families are safe. Is there a way to realize true peace and safety in our lives?

The answer is a resounding, "Yes!"

We can actually come to know the Prince of Peace, Jesus. He can give us peace no matter what chaos is going on around us.

And as to safety, there is a word in the Hebrew language that translates in English to salvation, safety.

That word is Yeshua, in English we say Jesus. In Him is all the safety in the world.

Yes, Jesus…peace and safety.

DAY 37

With the opening of the first two seals, the first two riders are revealed. The white horse carries the antichrist, and the red horse unleashes mass annihilation.

These prophecies are devastating enough, but there is yet more. *"When the Lamb opened the third seal, I heard the third living creature say, 'Come!' I looked, and there before me was a black horse! Its rider was holding a pair of scales in his hand. Then I heard what sounded like a voice among the four living creatures, saying, 'Two pounds of wheat for a day's wages, and six pounds of barley for a day's wages, and do not damage the oil and the wine!'"* Revelation 6:5-6

The rider of this black horse brings famine.

Before we go on, let's define some terms. The Greek word here for pound is choenix and it is equal to 1.92 pints. That amount therefore would weigh about two pounds. Then in Greek, we have the word denarius used in some translations for the price of barley or wheat. In Matthew 20 it was the amount paid for a day's wages.

This Revelation passage shows us that food will be scarce enough that a day's rations will cost a day's salary.

Over the last several years, we have seen food and commodity shortages. People have been furloughed or lost their jobs. The stock market has fluctuated, sometimes making severe changes. Supplies have lessened but so have wages. And we've seen it all in a few short years.

Does this mean that the third seal has already opened?

No.

This has been a taste of what is to come. Recent events have proven how quickly things can change. There is great blessing in that. God has given us a glimpse of what is on the horizon with time to get our lives ready.

How much time?

Good question!

We don't know. We only have assurance of this moment, right now. That is why today is the day of salvation.

When this third seal is opened, devastation will come and will be more challenging than anything we have yet experienced in our lifetime. In days past it's been easy to see how pandemics, floods, droughts, locusts, fires, wars can all play a part in food shortages and economic collapse.

And we've seen that it can happen almost overnight.

Do you remember that during the coronavirus pandemic, cash in some places was refused. It felt tainted and could possibly pass the disease. Even credit and debit cards were handled with gloves.

This gave us a glimpse of a coming time when people will not be able to buy or sell without an endorsed identification number, something that will be safe to scan maybe like on a hand or forehead. Right now, plans are in place globally for digital ID's.

Verse 6 of Revelation 6 comes with a warning, *"...and do not damage the oil and the wine." Revelation 6:6*

Some have said that this is referring to wealth. It may well be since food will cost so much.

It could also be referencing olive and grape harvests, in other words, farming, food production. Some years ago, there was great concern over an anomaly called Colony Collapse Syndrome. Bees were leaving hives for no known reason and the result was that a once thriving colony would abruptly end. Farmers and agriculturists saw this as a huge problem because so many of the world's crops must be pollinated by bees. In June of 2020, over 50 million bees were found dead in Croatia causing the country to declare a disaster. And another phenomenon has been a type of bees referred to as murder hornets that have gone in and decimated hives in a matter of hours.

According to statistics here in the United States one of every four bites of food we take is a result of bee pollination. Decline of bee populations results in far less food. During the end times will this situation with bees only get worse? Or will there be something else that causes people to plant, but not be able to reap? Could it be that seeds will be so genetically engineered that the food they produce is of little nutritional value or even inedible?

Or might this warning be referring to crude oil and product sales? Perhaps. We can't definitively say, but what we do see with the opening of this seal is famine. It's going to be global, and it's going to be terrible. People will turn against each other to get food.

When famine comes and people are starving, they will eat almost anything.

But there is yet an even more dangerous kind of famine. *In Amos 8:11 we read, "'The days are coming,' declares the Sovereign Lord, 'when I will send a famine through the land—not a famine of food or a thirst for water, but a famine of hearing the words of the Lord.'"*

Today we still have the opportunity to hear. Let's make sure we are listening.

Because when a famine of God's Word comes, people will believe almost anything.

DAY 38

With the opening of the first three seals, the antichrist, annihilation, and global food shortages have been unleashed. Yet, there is one more rider. He makes the fourth horseman of the Apocalypse.

"When the Lamb opened the fourth seal, I heard the voice of the fourth living creature say, 'Come!' I looked, and there before me was a pale horse! Its rider was named Death, and Hades was following close behind him. They were given power over a fourth of the earth to kill by sword, famine and plague, and by the wild beasts of the earth." Revelation 6:7-8

The rider is identified. His name is Death and he rides a pale horse. The Greek word here for pale is chlóros. It is a sickening green color. As unappealing as this might be, it denotes the color of regurgitation. But this rider is not alone. Death comes and then Hades follows. Hades is another word for hell.

These two are companions, death of the body and death of the soul.

Let's face it, the last few years have been scary. Death has been front and center as coronavirus swept our world. People died. Lots of them. We've also seen violence, murder, and war increase. But it's going to get worse.

In Revelation 6:7-8, it says that Death and Hades have power over one fourth of the earth. That could possibly be referring to geographic regions, but it could also mean population. Currently the population is at about eight billion people. We've already discussed that when the rapture takes place many people will suddenly be gone.

How many people will be left? That is an answer only the Lord knows. But it will still most likely number several billion.

So, if one fourth of the population is killed, it could mean millions will meet Death face-to-face, and Hades will be the pallbearer to take their souls to hell.

The tactics for this mass death seem to be the ramping-up of the destruction by the first three riders. Sword, famine, and plague are going to come in even more waves. Then another death threat is added, wild beasts. These could be any type of animal. Birds, land animals, and sea creatures may turn toward humans as prey. Because of famine, food shortages may be so severe that even pets, at a critical point of starvation, will turn against their owners and attack. But beasts might also refer to the microscopic, those beings that are beastly or brutal in nature, the ones that bring pandemics and plagues worse than anything we have yet seen.

The results of the unsealing of this pale horse rider will be massive amounts of Death with Hades following close behind.

The word used here is Hades, again another name for hell. This same place could be referred to in the Scripture as Gehenna, torment, the Abyss, or lake of fire.

Sadly, the concept of hell is debated. There are people who think that hell does not exist. The belief is that a loving God would never send someone to such a terrible place. This idea has wormed its way into modern day thinking. This idea has wormed its way into the church.

So, let's look at some truths from the Scripture.

One is that God absolutely is loving. 1 John 4:8 tells us that God is Himself, love. Everything He does is motivated by His overwhelming love for His creation, us.

Second, we have within us an eternal spirit. *Genesis 2:7* says, *"Then the Lord God formed a man from the dust of the ground and breathed into his nostrils the breath of life, and the man became a living being."* God put His breath into us. Nothing about God can be destroyed, so be assured we are going to live eternally. Physical death is the gateway to eternity.

Third, because the Lord loves us, He gives us a choice. We can choose Him, or we can choose our own way. If we decide we don't want to have Jesus in our lives, He does not force His way in. But what it also means is that if we make the choice to reject Christ, we will then live eternally away from Him. God does not send people to hell; people make the choice to live without the Lord.

Let there be no doubt, hell is a very real place. The Bible identifies it...Luke 12, Luke 16, Revelation 20. Since we are eternal beings, it means we are going to live someplace and there are only two options. Jesus offers life, but if that is rejected then a place that is the opposite is the result.

Hell is the place where the Lord isn't, so...

Hell is a bottomless pit because Jesus is the only firm foundation.

Hell is a place of torment. Jesus is healing and rest.

Hell is a place of agony. Jesus is peace.

Hell is a place of unquenchable thirst. Jesus is living water.

Hell is a place of blackest darkness. Jesus is the light of the world.

Hell is the second death eternally. Jesus is eternal life.

Hell is eternal punishment for our sin if we reject the Lord's offer of salvation. Jesus paid for our sin so we can accept His offer of salvation.

Hell is the residence of the father of lies. Jesus is truth.

Hell is hell because Jesus isn't there.

Choose Jesus today.

DAY 39

Yes, God is loving, but because of His great overwhelming love, He gives us a choice. If we reject Christ, we will live forever away from Him. If we choose the Lord, we get everything that He is. This means we need to be very careful about our choices. Our eternal lives depend on it.

Isaiah 66 and Mark 9 reference a place. It says in that place, their worm does not die and the fire is not quenched.

What is the place the two passages refer to?

This place is hell, where their worm doesn't die, and the fire is not quenched.

We understand the part about the fire, but what does the reference to the worm mean?

Let's examine that. We'll start by talking about worms.

This may not be considered a fact, but it is a strong opinion, worms are ugly creatures. Okay, maybe not among other worms, and yes, there is a place for them. They make good fish bait. They break up, aerate, and fertilize soil. They are the farmer's and fisherman's friend. But as far as beauty goes, they fall into the category of "not so much".

There is one in Israel that doesn't even come up to the lowly worm's standard of beauty. Even for a worm, this one is ugly. In fact, it barely looks like a worm. At first glance, one could easily mistake it for a growth on a tree. But ugly or not, it has a huge mission and purpose.

This worm is called the tola'at shani, the crimson worm, and it is an amazing creature. It is from this ugly little worm that the crimson dye for the Temple was made. That in itself makes it very special, but there is more.

When it's time for the female to lay eggs, she climbs onto a tree and attaches herself to the wood so firmly that to remove her would tear her body. Her eggs hatch and the tiny worms have a choice, they can wander away or they can feed on her flesh. She willingly gives her life so her children can live.

As they are feeding, she releases a crimson dye, her blood. It covers her offspring, and they are stained with it for the rest of their lives. It never washes away, and it never fades.

After three days, the mother worm curls up into a heart shape and her waxen body falls to the ground, as white as snow.

Do you see it? This homely little worm paints a beautiful picture.

Psalm 22 is a prophetic Psalm about the crucifixion. *Verse 6* says, *"But I am a worm and not a man, scorned by everyone, despised by the people."*

The worm in this verse is the tola'at shani, the crimson worm.

Like this worm, Jesus was not considered beautiful. Isaiah 53 tells us that there was nothing in His appearance to attract us to Him. But beautiful or not, Jesus came with a huge mission and purpose. He came to give His life.

He was nailed to the wood of the cross so firmly that to take Him down would tear His body. He willingly gave His life for us.

John 6:53-54 says, *"Very truly I tell you, unless you eat the flesh of the Son of Man and drink His blood, you have no life in you. Whoever eats my flesh and drinks my blood has eternal life, and I will raise them up at the last day."*

We have a choice. We can wander away or make the decision to receive Him. If we wander away, we will die an eternal death.

Just like those tiny worms need their mother's flesh to have life, we need to receive the Lord Jesus to have life. And just like those tiny worms are marked by their mother's blood, Jesus covers us with His blood, and it is never washed away, and it never fades or perishes.

Psalm 22:14, "I am poured out like water, and all my bones are out of joint. My heart has turned to wax; it has melted within me."

From hundreds of years prior to Jesus' dying on the cross, a tiny worm was portraying His death, His heart, His life-giving sacrifice for us. It says in *Isaiah 1:18, "…Though your sins are like scarlet, they shall be as white as snow…"*

Psalm 22 prophesied that Jesus would be just like that crimson worm, evidence that even the tiniest, most seemingly insignificant detail of the Scripture is proof positive of its truth.

Jesus is the One Psalm 22 is referring to.

The worm, the tola'at shani, is a picture of Jesus who died for us. We can accept His sacrifice and become one of His children.

But in hell that sacrifice has been rejected, so their worm never dies.

DAY 40

Sadly, many people reject Christ. But for some that's not enough, they won't be satisfied until Christianity is stamped out altogether. Persecution began in the first century when Stephen was stoned to death. That set off a firestorm of trying to completely wipe out Christianity.

That same attitude has persisted around the world and goes on until today. Every day, believers face the fear of persecution and death. Millions have been martyred for their faith. God's persecuted people are in many nations. Some are dying, some are being tortured, some are imprisoned.

The church is Jesus' bride, and one day, (and it looks like it could be very soon), He is going to come to snatch His bride away.

Let's review. People refer to that event as the rapture. The word used in 1 Thessalonians is harpazó, it means snatched or caught up.

"Brothers and sisters, we do not want you to be uninformed about those who sleep in death, so that you do not grieve like the rest of mankind, who have no hope. For we believe that Jesus died and rose again, and so we believe that God will bring with Jesus those who have fallen asleep in him. According to the Lord's word, we tell you that we who are still alive, who are left until the coming of the Lord, will certainly not precede those who have fallen asleep. For the Lord himself will come down from heaven, with a loud command, with the voice of the archangel and with the trumpet call of God, and the dead in Christ will rise first. After that, we who are still alive and are left will be caught up together with them in the clouds to meet the Lord

in the air. And so we will be with the Lord forever. Therefore encourage one another with these words." 1 Thessalonians 4:13-18

Believers will suddenly be gone. The Bible says it will happen in the twinkling of an eye. How fast that will be is almost incalculable. It literally means we will be here and immediately we will be with Him.

After that event people will be left behind. Some will become Christ followers, but it is going to be a very challenging time. During the seven years of the tribulation, the devil's goal will be to rule. He hates Christians now. He will hate with a vengeance during that time. Christians' lives will be in constant grave danger. Many will be killed for their faith. They will stand against the antichrist, by standing for Jesus. So as the fifth seal is opened, it unveils persecution and death for tribulation believers.

Those who have prayed to receive Christ after the rapture takes place will face death. Each morning they may wake up to the question, "Lord, is today the day my life ends?" Each night they may lie down wondering whether someone will come and awaken them to march them off to a death camp. Because many of those tribulation believers will indeed die.

We see their souls awaiting God's vengeance as the fifth seal is opened. *"When he opened the fifth seal, I saw under the altar the souls of those who had been slain because of the word of God and the testimony they had maintained. They called out in a loud voice, 'How long, Sovereign Lord, holy and true, until you judge the inhabitants of the earth and avenge our blood?' Then each of them was given a white robe, and they were told to wait a little longer, until the full number of their fellow servants, their brothers and sisters, were killed just as they had been." Revelation 6:9-11*

God alone knows how long the killing spree of those tribulation saints will be.

God alone knows how many will die.

God alone knows how and when they will be avenged.

It is a terrible picture, and yet not one bit of it is outside the hands of the Lord. He's got it all in His control.

They are given white robes, a picture of being covered in Christ's righteousness and told to wait. Their pain is over, their suffering behind them, but they must be patient a little longer until such a time as God deals with those who have caused their suffering.

The martyrdom of the saints is awful. Taking someone's life is one of the most horrible crimes against a person. But death is not the worst thing. The ones spoken of in this passage are believers, people who love and follow Jesus. Their lives will end here, but their real lives will begin at the heavenly altar of the Lord, clothed in the righteousness of Christ.

The saddest, most awful truth is for those people who are doling out the terror. They made their decisions to follow Satan's plan. Perhaps for a few more days, weeks, or even a couple more years, they will live on the earth. But then they too will die and as soon as their earthly lives are over, their real lives will begin, and they will be in terror and torment for eternity.

Matthew 10:28, "Do not be afraid of those who kill the body but cannot kill the soul. Rather, be afraid of the One who can destroy both soul and body in hell."

DAY 41

Remember hearing these words, "This is unprecedented."

And it was. Things that we had never experienced before became common place. A pandemic changed our known world. Yet historically, there have been pandemics. The Bubonic plague, the Spanish flu, the Ebola outbreak have all appeared before coronavirus made its debut. So, we have had some frame of reference when it comes to outbreaks of diseases.

But these next verses show us things unlike anything we can even begin to comprehend.

"I watched as he opened the sixth seal. There was a great earthquake. The sun turned black like sackcloth made of goat hair, the whole moon turned blood red, and the stars in the sky fell to earth, as figs drop from a fig tree when shaken by a strong wind. The heavens receded like a scroll being rolled up, and every mountain and island was removed from its place." Revelation 6:12-14

The words, "This is unprecedented" certainly apply here.

The closest comparison for this description is a nuclear explosion. But as we read that every mountain, every island is removed from its place, this indicates a global event with a massive earthquake, the sun blackening, the moon turning red, stars falling, and the heavens receding. Imagine John trying to wrap his mind around what the Lord allowed him to see. It must have been horrific. John would have never seen anything before like what he was seeing. Words would have been hard to formulate except that God told him how to describe it.

Most of us have seen pictures and film of atomic and nuclear explosions, but this description in Revelation goes way beyond that.

Will it be calderas and volcanoes around the world suddenly erupting and exploding simultaneously that cause burning volcanic debris to fall back to the earth like figs dropping from the trees?

Will it be bombs and instruments of war waged against the entire world?

Will it be a meteor storm that causes massive destruction along with fires, earthquakes, and so much ash rising that the sun is darkened, and the moon turns blood red?

Or could it be some type of massive cataclysmic airburst?

What will this be?

We don't know.

It is the opening of the sixth seal and what we do know, is that it is beyond our comprehension as to how terrible this will be.

"Then the kings of the earth, the princes, the generals, the rich, the mighty, and everyone else, both slave and free, hid in caves and among the rocks of the mountains. They called to the mountains and the rocks, 'Fall on us and hide us from the face of him who sits on the throne and from the wrath of the Lamb! For the great day of their wrath has come, and who can withstand it?'" Revelation 6:15-17

When this sixth seal is opened and the massive destruction comes, the world leaders along with everyone else will run. They will try to hide in caves and among the debris from the toppled mountains. But what is so terrible is that they realize that this is the wrath of the Lamb of God being poured out, but they do not repent. They understand that this comes from God, but rather than calling out to the Lord of Hosts, they cry out to the rocks to be saved from the devastation.

Let's reiterate that.

They cry out to rocks!

Imagine. They know Who is in charge. They have the full realization that what is happening in the world is coming from the Lamb. But their hearts are so hard, so far from God that they call out to rocks.

How did their hearts get so hardened? Perhaps days, weeks, or even years before, an invitation was given to receive Christ and accept the truth of the Bible. Jesus knocked on the door of the person's heart and they refused. The Lord may have come again, but with each refusal the heart began to turn from a heart of flesh into a heart of stone. In the book of Exodus, Pharaoh was like that. Time and time again, God offered Him signs to turn his heart. Time and time again, Pharaoh refused to listen. His heart became so hard that he could no longer even see or understand truth. He sank in the Red Sea and drowned.

In the book of Revelation, the people cry out to rocks. When we are in trouble where do we turn?

This moment, as we read the passage, let's realize that there is only one place where we can go when we are in trouble.

"God is our refuge and strength, an ever-present help in trouble." *Psalm 46:1*

REVELATION

CHAPTER 7

DAY 42

"After this I saw four angels standing at the four corners of the earth, holding back the four winds of the earth to prevent any wind from blowing on the land or on the sea or on any tree." Revelation 7:1

First, lest there be any question about the power God has given to angels, look at this. It only takes four of them to hold back every bit of wind on the planet. In our world today, there is always wind somewhere, even if where we are is calm. This will be an unprecedented moment in time, zero wind on the entire earth. Why?

One of the reasons may be that this is the calm after the storm of the first six seals, and the calm before the next storm with another series of judgments. Six of the seven seals have been broken and the judgments poured out on the earth. Then there is this brief pause. This same pattern also occurs with the trumpet judgments that are coming. As chapter 7 begins, God brings a quiet stillness to the entire planet. There is no wind anywhere. These four angels hold back the wind on the land, the sea, and even the trees.

God is love so what God does, He does out of a heart of love. Every judgment that is poured out is designed to bring people to an understanding that He is the Lord. He is God, and He is absolutely in charge of this world.

We see this in the Old Testament with the plagues poured out on Egypt. God was calling Pharaoh to soften his heart. Pharaoh was unyielding, so the plagues got bigger and louder.

God wants every one of us to see that every second of a life apart from Him is worthless, chaotic, and filled with uncertainty.

In Revelation God sends the first set of judgments.

But now as chapter 7 begins, God brings a few moments of stillness for the world to ponder the judgments that have happened, and those still to come.

Psalm 46:10 tells us to be still and know that He is God. Here the storm has passed and this stillness covering the world speaks.

When there is a calm, use it to think about who God is, how powerful He is, and how much He wants us to turn to Him.

When there is a storm, use it to think about who God is, how powerful He is, and how much He wants us to turn to Him.

In the chaos or the stillness, turn to Him.

"Then I saw another angel coming up from the east, having the seal of the living God. He called out in a loud voice to the four angels who had been given power to harm the land and the sea: 'Do not harm the land or the sea or the trees until we put a seal on the foreheads of the servants of our God.' Then I heard the number of those who were sealed: 144,000 from all the tribes of Israel. From the tribe of Judah 12,000 were sealed, from the tribe of Reuben 12,000, from the tribe of Gad 12,000, from the tribe of Asher 12,000, from the tribe of Naphtali 12,000, from the tribe of Manasseh 12,000, from the tribe of Simeon 12,000, from the tribe of Levi 12,000, from the tribe of Issachar 12,000, from the tribe of Zebulun 12,000, from the tribe of Joseph 12,000, from the tribe of Benjamin 12,000." Revelation 7:2-8

Signed, sealed, delivered, 144,000 from the tribes of Israel. They will be set apart for special service to God and given special protection by God. We don't know exactly what their job will be. I like to think of them as an army of Apostle Paul's. I think he was perhaps the prototype for these guys. If we jump ahead to chapter 14, we can read a short description of who these servants are, so we will delve into this a little more when we get to that passage.

But we know from this chapter that God placed His seal on their foreheads. Nothing, NOTHING, in all of life can compare to God placing His mark on us, saying we belong to Him.

There is nothing more beautiful, nothing more powerful, no place more secure.

And the good news is that this isn't just for them sometime in the future. Ephesians 4:30 tells us that for all of us who are believers, we have been sealed by the Holy Spirit for the day of redemption.

There is nothing more beautiful, more powerful, more secure.

Signed, sealed, and someday delivered into the arms of Jesus.

Let's look a little deeper at this list.

There are twelve tribes of Israel named here.

Why these?

Why the order that they are in?

This is not the birth order of the sons of Jacob. Manasseh and Ephraim were the two sons of Joseph, not part of the original twelve sons, so why is Manasseh in this group? Why is Dan not listed? And those are all good questions. When we have these questions, we need to stop, pause, and ask if there might be something hidden for us to uncover. This is what the rabbis call a remez, a mystery. And don't you just love a good mystery? I went back to Genesis to see what was said at the birth of each of these sons. See if these words might be an incredible blessing as we read this simple list of names.

Judah-I will praise the Lord

Reuben-Because the Lord has seen my misery

Gad-What good fortune

Asher-The women will call me happy

Naphtali-I have had a great struggle

Manasseh-God has made me forget all my trouble

Simeon-Because the Lord heard that I am not loved

Levi-Now my husband will become attached to me

Issachar-God has rewarded me

Zebulun-My husband will treat me with honor

Joseph-May the Lord add to me another son

Benjamin-The son of my right hand

Hmm, aren't those phrases interesting and impactful in that order? Let's read it together now without the names and with a couple of connecting words:

I will praise the Lord because the Lord has seen my misery. What good fortune; the women will call me happy. I have had a great struggle. God has made me forget all my trouble because the Lord heard that I am not loved. Now, my husband will become attached to me. God has rewarded me. My husband will treat me with honor. May the Lord add to me another son, the son of my right hand.

Israel had entered a covenant with the Lord. In essence, God took Israel into a partnership like that of husband and wife. However, as we read the Old Testament, we see the unfaithfulness of Israel. In the book of Hosea, we read about an unfaithful wife, Gomer. It is the picture of this wayward nation, Israel. Just like Gomer, Israel strayed away from the Lord. But here, in the book of Revelation, the Lord, the Husband, is bringing them back. They will see His love and recognize that they need the Son who is now seated at the right hand of God.

A list of names, but an incredible message.

DAY 43

I have had the great joy several times of being a part of a crowd of worshipers that topped ten thousand. I witnessed an event on TV where a million men gathered in Washington DC for prayer and teaching. It was beyond words. I fell to my knees as tears streamed down my face.

But this? Wow!

"After this I looked, and there before me was a great multitude that no one could count, from every nation, tribe, people and language, standing before the throne and before the Lamb. They were wearing white robes and were holding palm branches in their hands. And they cried out in a loud voice: 'Salvation belongs to our God, who sits on the throne, and to the Lamb.' All the angels were standing around the throne and around the elders and the four living creatures. They fell down on their faces before the throne and worshiped God, saying: 'Amen! Praise and glory and wisdom and thanks and honor and power and strength be to our God for ever and ever. Amen!'" Revelation 7:9-12

Remember, John had been living out his exile on the island of Patmos when suddenly the Lord called him up to heaven for a panoramic view of the future. John was given the distinct privilege of seeing and hearing and writing all that he saw. And here he saw a great multitude, more than anyone could count. Thousands upon thousands, ten thousand times ten thousand, we don't know how many, but this is most certainly the biggest worship event in all of history.

Angels filled the night sky when Jesus was born, and their praise filled the heavens. Here all the angels are joined with people from every tribe, nation, tongue, people group. What a scene!

This morning, as I am studying this, tears fill my eyes just thinking about this glorious moment. It will be beyond spectacular, beyond anything we have ever known about worship. And for all of us who know the Lord, I believe that we will get to be a part of this amazing celebration. We will be among those who are in that multitude.

I wonder, as John was transported to this future event, did he happen to catch a glimpse of any of us standing there?

And then these words: *"Amen! Praise and glory and wisdom and thanks and honor and power and strength be to our God for ever and ever. Amen!" Revelation 7:12*

Praise, glory, wisdom, thanks, honor, power, strength…how many words do these worshipers in heaven use? And of course, the answer is seven. That doesn't mean that there aren't more, we can think of hundreds. But seven is a number of completeness, so this is worship at its absolute best.

Angels, elders, living creatures, and a great multitude, all worshiping in harmony, all giving praise to God, all singing at the top of their lungs, His praises.

When does your heart explode with adoration? When does praise just naturally flow out of you? What causes you to worship?

Is it in nature? The mountains, the oceans, the rivers, the fall colors, the spring flowers, when you look at the beauty of the world that God made, does your heart soar with the glory of it all and your lips burst forth with praise?

How about when you hear music? Does the song swell within you until you can't help but burst into song right along with the music?

Is it when you look into the face of a newborn child or grandchild and thank the Lord for this gift?

Maybe it's when you are just sitting quietly in the presence of Almighty God, talking with Him and basking in His goodness, faithfulness, sweetness, love, and compassion.

Perhaps, it is in the middle of studying His Word. When He speaks directly to you and you know that you have had an encounter with the Creator of the entire universe, is that when worship erupts out of you?

Most probably it is all these things that inspire us to worship.

"Amen! Praise and glory and wisdom and thanks and honor and power and strength be to our God for ever and ever. Amen!"

What a gift that we get to join the worship now!

DAY 44

My husband has occasionally been interviewed by the news. It has sometimes been about an event he was coordinating, but there have also been some "man on the street" questions when he has been in the right place at the right time.

These verses begin with a bit of the "man on the street" interview. But this question comes from one of the twenty-four elders. They have a heavenly perspective. John has an interesting answer.

"Then one of the elders asked me, 'These in white robes—who are they, and where did they come from?' I answered, 'Sir, you know.' And he said, 'These are they who have come out of the great tribulation; they have washed their robes and made them white in the blood of the Lamb. Therefore, they are before the throne of God and serve him day and night in his temple; and he who sits on the throne will shelter them with his presence. Never again will they hunger; never again will they thirst. The sun will not beat down on them, nor any scorching heat. For the Lamb at the center of the throne will be their shepherd; he will lead them to springs of living water. And God will wipe away every tear from their eyes.'" Revelation 7:13-17

Who are these elders?

What we know is that there are twenty-four of them. Scholars have speculated. Some say people from both the Old and New Testaments. It's possible that twelve of them could be from the twelve tribes of Israel. Then another twelve could be the disciples, perhaps Matthias rather than Judas, or maybe Paul in place of Judas. Some scholars say this number could be symbolic of all believers in heaven.

Here's the thing, we don't yet know. And that is okay. We have this to look forward to, there will be new and exciting things to learn and discover in heaven.

Who makes up this great multitude? What we know from this chapter of Scripture is they come from every tribe, nation, language, and people. They wear white robes. They hold palm branches. They praise God. And John gets asked a question about them from one of the elders.

"These in white robes—who are they, and where did they come from?"

And John answers a lot like we probably would, *"Sir, you know."* And then the answer was given.

It was enough of an answer for John, and for the time being it has to be enough of an answer for us. They have come out of the great tribulation. Some think this could mean tribulation and persecution for believers since the beginning, some just during the last years. Were they raptured, or martyred, or just died? It's not yet clear, but it is enough because what we see is that no matter how or when they arrived in heaven, they have arrived, and the Lamb is taking the most glorious care of them.

And that is a blessed hope for us. No matter how or when we arrive in heaven, Jesus, the Lamb, will be there to guarantee our safety and refreshment and give us a newfound joy.

Amen!

REVELATION
CHAPTER 8

DAY 45

"*When he opened the seventh seal, there was silence in heaven for about half an hour.*" *Revelation 8:1*

It is impossible for us to understand this dramatic incredible thirty minutes of time. Up to this point, worship and praise and adoration have been the beautiful tone of heaven, but as this seal is opened, there is complete silence. God is about to move in such a powerful way that everything ceases.

We very rarely experience complete silence. As I am writing this, it is 3:30 AM. I am alone in my living room. The TV is not on. I am not playing music and yet my world is not silent. When it rains, I can hear it hitting my roof. Sometimes there is thunder in the background. I can often hear birds singing. But even if that were not the case, there is the slight hum of my furnace or air conditioner, a few cars on the street, the ice dropping from my icemaker. My world is not silent.

This verse says there will be silence in heaven indicating that something incredibly profound is about to take place. This silence is speaking; it is telling the world to get ready. Complete silence demands attention.

It is important that we take the time to become silent before the Lord.

It is often in silence that we hear the best. *Psalm 46:10* gives us that directive.

"*He says, 'Be still, and know that I am God; I will be exalted among the nations, I will be exalted in the earth.'*"

We need to take time, become silent, open His Word, and as we read, listen to what He is saying.

And then we see the reason for the silence.

"And I saw the seven angels who stand before God, and seven trumpets were given to them." Revelation 8:2

Repeatedly in this mysterious, challenging, at times frightening, unveiling of future events, we see the number seven. In just this verse, we see seven angels and seven trumpets. These angels will sound the trumpets and events will roll out that bring great despair to many. But we want to be reminded that the number seven is God's number.

He has revealed the future before it will happen. He will be in the middle of it while it is happening. He will be there after it takes place. Yes, this is a time of judgment, but God is present even in judgment.

Jesus is with us, no matter what we face. He is at the beginning, in the middle, at the end.

It is even one of His names, the Alpha and the Omega, the beginning and the end.

"Another angel, who had a golden censer, came and stood at the altar. He was given much incense to offer, with the prayers of all God's people, on the golden altar in front of the throne." Revelation 8:3

I'm not sure where the image originated, but again, many people view angels as tiny babies with wings. That's a cute picture but so very far from the Biblical truth of angels. They are warriors. They are powerful. They are worshipers. They are musicians. They have a mission.

An angel comes and stands at the altar. He brings incense with the prayers of God's people to the altar before the throne. His mission is to carry those prayers to the throne of God.

Sometimes it feels as if our prayers only hit the ceiling. But remember, it does not matter how it feels when we pray. What matters is what the truth is when we pray. The truth for God's people is that our prayers are carried before the Lord.

Our prayers are heard. He hears. We must never forget; He hears us when we pray.

And there is a response to the prayers

"The smoke of the incense, together with the prayers of God's people, went up before God from the angel's hand. Then the angel took the censer, filled it with fire from the altar, and hurled it on the earth; and there came peals of thunder, rumblings, flashes of lightning and an earthquake." Revelation 8:4-5

As the prayers are lifted to God, fire, thunder, lightning, and an earthquake are hurled down to the earth.

That's quite a response to the prayers. It may not seem like the answers we actually want from our prayers, does it? We want peace, healing, recovery, a gentle answer. But we must always remember that the Lord knows exactly what we as individuals and as a world need. We want a whisper but there are times when He knows we need a shout.

That is what we see in Revelation. It is the double-edged sword. He brings both grace and judgment. This book is filled with His judgment. But that is what people will need in order to see.

It works that way today also. There are many who respond to the call to repent and come to Christ after hearing about His great love for them in a Sunday morning message. But there are also many who cannot be interrupted by a message of grace and will only hear when their lives are interrupted by some type of pain or loss. God uses both sides of the sword.

One day we will understand and see that all of it has come from a heart of love. A love that is so great, it will use any means possible to reach as many as possible.

So, what will it take for us? The gentle call of grace or the painful call of judgment?

DAY 46

Do you remember during the shutdown across the country people were linking being a couch potato with patriotism? I have to guess that was the first time in our history when it seemed appropriate to link doing absolutely nothing with being a good American. One of the building blocks of our country has been hard work, and it's refreshing to see that we are now well past couch potato being red, white, and blue.

From the very beginning of time, God intended for us to work. He put Adam in the garden and directed him to work the land. Work is a blessing.

We need to ask what it is that the Lord wants each of us to do today.

We see in the Scripture passage in heaven there are tasks to perform. Even the angels have jobs.

"Then the seven angels who had the seven trumpets prepared to sound them." Revelation 8:6

Each of these angels is going to sound a trumpet. A plague or pandemic, unlike anything the world has ever seen, will sweep across the globe. God knows, at that time, it is what it will take in order for people to look up. God will do whatever it takes to reach as many as possible.

Right now, we have opportunities to work for Him. What does He want us to do to reach as many as possible?

"The first angel sounded his trumpet, and there came hail and fire mixed with blood, and it was hurled down on the earth. A third of the earth

was burned up, a third of the trees were burned up, and all the green grass was burned up." Revelation 8:7

It is part of our nature that we want, what we want, when we want it. When we go that direction, away from God, He will do whatever He can to reach our hearts to draw us to Himself.

We see in this verse that as the first angel sounds his trumpet, hail and fire overtake the earth. One third of the earth, trees, and grass are completely burned up. The world stands back and sees much of what they have worked for go up in smoke. Where do you turn when everything is gone?

That is the choice the Lord is giving. The choice is to turn to Him in repentance and use our time to serve Him. Or we can cross our arms, get angry, and determine to somehow solve it ourselves. Here in the book of Revelation we see that many choose the latter. And what people will see during this time of tribulation, is that no self-determination, fix-it-yourself, pull yourself up by the bootstraps will work. The only hope is in Jesus.

Actually, Jesus has always been the only hope during any time.

But the judgment isn't done.

"The second angel sounded his trumpet, and something like a huge mountain, all ablaze, was thrown into the sea. A third of the sea turned into blood, a third of the living creatures in the sea died, and a third of the ships were destroyed." Revelation 8:8-9

When the first angel sounds his trumpet, a third of the earth is burned up. With this second trumpet, we see a third of the sea is destroyed.

It is impossible to identify the cause at this point.

A meteor? Possibly.

A volcanic eruption? It could be.

A third of the sea turns to blood.

Is this actual blood? Probably, but it could also be the phenomenon seen in recent years called "red tide." Red tide is an organism that multiplies at such an alarming rate that it turns the water blood red and kills sea life. This time it is not localized but is global and affects one third of the waters. But it could also be something completely unknown until the moment it happens.

What we do know is that a blazing mountain falls into the sea and one third of all water creatures and ships are destroyed.

What is the loss of life?

What is the financial loss?

What kind of fear invades?

What kind of anger takes over?

Is this judgment? Yes, but it is still God's call to repent and experience eternity with Him.

We can listen now as He is calling in His loving grace. We appeal to you...don't wait.

DAY 47

Sirens blaring at 2:30 in the morning, jarring us out of our much-needed sleep, could be looked at as just a terrible annoyance, or we could see it for what it is, a wake-up call to danger approaching.

The warnings in Revelation are the wake-up call to the danger coming on the world.

"The third angel sounded his trumpet, and a great star, blazing like a torch, fell from the sky on a third of the rivers and on the springs of water— the name of the star is Wormwood. A third of the waters turned bitter, and many people died from the waters that had become bitter." Revelation 8:10-11

Death is going to come as a result of this star, blazing like a torch, falling into the rivers and springs. It does not tell us of the loss of life because of the collision, but it does tell us of the loss of life due to drinking the polluted waters. Many people will die.

This may point to an asteroid that comes hurtling through the atmosphere and makes a land strike. It could well be pieces that break apart over numerous springs and rivers. We cannot be certain exactly what this event includes, but we can understand the clear message. Death comes. This star is named Wormwood.

That name comes from a bitter herb that can be fatal if ingested in the wrong amount. We see that after this star strikes, the waters become bitter and are undrinkable. One third of the water is literally poisoned.

It's impossible to know exactly how this will play out.

Is there an asteroid headed to the earth that will create this scenario? Could a flaming star spew out debris over our rivers and springs?

Perhaps.

April 26, 1986, an accident at a nuclear power plant caused by a chain reaction, released airborne radioactive particles throughout the area. It became known as the worst nuclear disaster in all of history. Russia and Western Europe were tragically affected. Evacuations, deaths, radiation burns...the cost, both monetarily and lives impacted, is incalculable.

The place?

Chernobyl.

The translation of this Ukrainian name?

Wormwood.

Could this event outlined in Revelation 8 be another nuclear disaster?

Certainly, it could.

Could the Chernobyl disaster be a warning of something far worse?

Possibly.

Again, it's impossible to know exactly how this will unfold.

We don't know the details yet of how this takes place. We probably won't know for sure until the world is in the midst of it.

But for now, it's enough to know that it will happen. It's certainly a good idea to live each day as if it is our last.

"The fourth angel sounded his trumpet, and a third of the sun was struck, a third of the moon, and a third of the stars, so that a third of them turned dark. A third of the day was without light, and also a third of the night." Revelation 8:12

Could this be from nuclear fallout?

Could there be some space calamity?

Could the tragic events that have already befallen planet earth create such a cloud cover that darkness reigns?

We have seen in our study of Revelation that we cannot nail down the specifics of the events outlined as John recorded them.

He was using first century language to record events scheduled for centuries in the future. But as it unfolds, it will be strikingly understandable that he recorded exactly what would take place. It is amazingly precise. Prophecy is one of the evidences that Scripture is completely accurate.

This passage warns us that a time is coming when the sun, moon, and stars are affected in such a way that their light is diminished by one third. It doesn't explain how or even what that actually means. It will make complete sense when it happens.

So, we aren't going to try to unwrap this event any more than what the passage says, but we are going to look for a takeaway.

Today, we have all the light we need to understand how to become a follower of Jesus, walk in faith, and live out the life He calls us to.

There is coming a time when it will be much harder to see. The earth will be covered by a period of darkness, but it will also be covered by a cloud of deception that is unequaled. It will be harder to understand and follow than at any other time.

We have the light today. Don't wait. Say yes to Jesus and walk in the light of His Word.

The Scripture then tells us what's next.

"As I watched, I heard an eagle that was flying in midair call out in a loud voice: 'Woe! Woe! Woe to the inhabitants of the earth, because of the trumpet blasts about to be sounded by the other three angels!'" Revelation 8:13

This chapter in Revelation has highlighted events that unfold, impacting one third of the earth in a number of different ways. Each of these scenarios has affected one third.

This verse also carries the number three. But today it is, "Woe! Woe! Woe!" These three "woes" carry a great warning. Something worse is coming, worse than anything the world has ever seen. As frightening, tragic, devastating, harmful as it has been, it is about to get worse. But God in His incredible love is issuing a warning. It's the tornado siren sounding. Look out. It's coming.

But it is not just there for those facing the very end of days. Those words were penned for all of us since God directed John to write them down.

"Woe! Woe! Woe to the inhabitants of the earth..." Things are going to get bad. Get ready.

He is telling us to get ready.

When?

Get ready now.

REVELATION

CHAPTER 9

DAY 48

"The fifth angel sounded his trumpet, and I saw a star that had fallen from the sky to the earth. The star was given the key to the shaft of the Abyss. When he opened the Abyss, smoke rose from it like the smoke from a gigantic furnace. The sun and sky were darkened by the smoke from the Abyss." Revelation 9:1-2

A star fell. So, what does this mean? In Revelation chapter one, the seven stars are angels. Isaiah 14 references a star that fell from heaven who wanted to be like the Most High yet was brought down.

Today's passage is most likely referring to an angel who also appears like a star.

This star in Revelation is given a key to open the shaft of the Abyss. It does not previously have the means to open it to unleash its horrible contents until the Lord's time is set in motion. It is God who has authority over all creation. Psalm 104 tells us that God rides a chariot of clouds on the winds, wraps Himself in light as a garment, makes the winds His messengers, and flames of fire His servants.

God spoke, and all of creation came to be. It is under His control. Creation bows to God's commands. In Matthew's Gospel, a star was pressed into service to lead wise men from far away to seek the Child, Jesus.

The star mentioned here in Revelation has no such lovely duty. His assignment is to open the Abyss.

Once again, let's affirm that the Abyss, hell, is a real place. There is unquenchable fire. When the shaft is opened the smoke that rises is so thick that the sky and the sun are darkened. But as the smoke rises, so does something else and what comes is terrifying.

In recent days, there have been plagues of locusts. They have devoured many of the crops in areas of Africa, India, and Pakistan. They have decimated acres upon acres of plants. These insects swoop in and strip the land of anything green. It has been said that recent plagues of locusts have been like nothing people have seen for decades.

In Bible days, we know that locusts came and did exactly what they have done in parts of the world today. John knew what locust plagues were. The word locusts was the word that God told him to use as he described what swarmed out of the Abyss.

"And out of the smoke locusts came down on the earth and were given power like that of scorpions of the earth. They were told not to harm the grass of the earth or any plant or tree, but only those people who did not have the seal of God on their foreheads. They were not allowed to kill them but only to torture them for five months. And the agony they suffered was like that of the sting of a scorpion when it strikes. During those days people will seek death but will not find it; they will long to die, but death will elude them." Revelation 9:3-6

Yes, locusts, but not like any locusts John had seen before. First, they had the stinging power of scorpions. I understand that the pain from a scorpion sting can be intense. The venom can cause anaphylaxis, so it's bad.

Second, the locusts in this passage do not target and eat what is green. They target people, a specific group, and they sting them like scorpions. The ones they go after are ones who do not have the seal of God on them. In Revelation 7, we discussed that God placed His seal on His followers. That seal then protects them from the attack of these Abyss locusts. This passage gives us a glimpse into the absolute misery the stings will cause for those without God's seal. It will last for five months and be so terrible that people will beg to die. Yet death will elude them.

The followers of God will be able to move freely with no fear of these terrible creatures. They will not be stung. But those who have chosen to follow the devil's plan will be in absolute agony.

Remember, when we come to Christ we too are sealed. In Paul's writing to the church at Ephesus he told them, *"...When you believed, you were marked in him with a seal, the promised Holy Spirit, who is a deposit guaranteeing our inheritance until the redemption of those who are God's possession—to the praise of his glory." Ephesians 1:13-14*

We may not be able to go to the mirror and see it, but if we are followers of the Lord Jesus, we have the seal. He protects and guides us. Talk about good news.

Does that mean that as Christians we don't ever face hard things? No, there are challenges and troubles in our world, and it will be magnified for those living during the tribulation time. But it does mean we are sealed by the Lord, so whatever we face, He leads us through it.

When we ended Revelation chapter 8, we read about an eagle flying in midair, and in a loud voice saying, *"Woe! Woe! Woe to the inhabitants of the earth..."*

Three woes.

These words are not merely an expression. They are announcements of three terrible major events. We have begun looking at the first woe. It is this plague of creatures described as locusts from the Abyss.

We're given even more description. *"The locusts looked like horses prepared for battle. On their heads they wore something like crowns of gold, and their faces resembled human faces. Their hair was like women's hair, and their teeth were like lions' teeth. They had breastplates like breastplates of iron, and the sound of their wings was like the thundering of many horses and chariots rushing into battle. They had tails with stingers, like scorpions, and in their tails they had power to torment people for five months. They had as king over them the angel of the Abyss, whose name in Hebrew is Abaddon and in Greek is Apollyon (that is, Destroyer). The first woe is past; two other woes are yet to come." Revelation 9:7-12*

Many scholars have tried to nail down exactly what these locusts are.

Some have suggested that the description is of a type of helicopter which sprays a toxin.

Perhaps they are a type of drone which can target individuals.

Others have said they are actual locusts but have mutated to look very different from anything we have ever seen. Recently we have seen different, scarier versions of insects. We've already mentioned those terrible murder hornets that are not like other bees. These things are cannibalistic, decapitating their honeybee victims. So, could these locusts be a much different, much scarier version of the insects?

Still others say the locusts mentioned here are demons. They certainly sound demonic and they rise out of the Abyss.

Whatever they are, their leader, their king, is the destroyer and they are horrific creatures. Again, let's emphasize that the torment these things bring will make death look preferable, and yet for five long months, people will not die, they will suffer terribly.

During this tribulation period, people will make an eternal choice, follow Christ, or follow Satan. Many will be deceived into thinking that the devil's plan will bring peace and prosperity on the earth. Utopia will appear to be within reach, but the devil is a liar. His plan is to steal, kill, and destroy. He pours out torture and torment on his followers. He has no compassion, no restraint. He is Abaddon in Hebrew, Apollyon in Greek, destroyer in English.

It seems unthinkable that anyone would choose this destroyer.

DAY 49

We sisters taught on "Seeing Christ in the Passover" and we were given a calendar as a gift. I know I am old-fashioned, or maybe I'm just old, but I can't get used to using my phone as a calendar. I like a hard copy. I want to be able to glance at the month all at once and see what's coming up. But even though I haven't had this paper calendar for too long, I've already made changes. Some things have been blotted out, and other things written in the space.

But God also has a calendar, and His calendar and ours are not the same. As I said, ours change. Appointments get cancelled, interruptions happen, closings halt our plans, emergencies move us quickly from one place to another with little time to prepare. But God is so precise, so perfect, that every detail down to the smallest has happened and will happen exactly as God has planned. Every single word of Revelation either has taken place, is taking place, or will take place precisely as the Lord has decreed it to be. There is nothing that can alter what God has said.

"The sixth angel sounded his trumpet, and I heard a voice coming from the four horns of the golden altar that is before God. It said to the sixth angel who had the trumpet, 'Release the four angels who are bound at the great river Euphrates.' And the four angels who had been kept ready for this very hour and day and month and year were released to kill a third of mankind. The number of the mounted troops was twice ten thousand times ten thousand. I heard their number." Revelation 9:13-16

A third of mankind will die by what comes from this release. Angels bound at the river Euphrates will be unbound.

Let's remember that demons were once angels that chose to follow the devil. Since they have been bound, the context leads us to believe that these are indeed demons. Their goal is to kill, and they will. They are being kept ready for a precise moment in time and it will happen at that very moment. But along with these will be an army of mounted troops. They are numbered. There are two hundred million of them. A force that size sounds almost impossible and yet China alone could have that large of an army. These will again be like nothing the world has ever experienced and the mounts they ride are creatures that are beyond our comprehension.

Again, let me emphasize that God's timing is perfect. Today we still have time to examine our lives and make changes. But soon, and based on what we see, very soon, the time clock for these events will strike and the countdown will begin.

Let's go back to look at that number again, *"twice ten thousand times ten thousand"*. That number is two hundred million and it's talking about an army.

Here's a little more description from *Revelation 9:17-19*. *"The horses and riders I saw in my vision looked like this: Their breastplates were fiery red, dark blue, and yellow as sulfur. The heads of the horses resembled the heads of lions, and out of their mouths came fire, smoke and sulfur. A third of mankind was killed by the three plagues of fire, smoke and sulfur that came out of their mouths. The power of the horses was in their mouths and in their tails; for their tails were like snakes, having heads with which they inflict injury."*

The breastplates appear to be some type of uniform covering. The colors are described, red, blue, yellow. Again, every detail in Scripture is given to us for a reason. Why these colors?

Fire, smoke, and sulfur come from the horses' mouths. The colors may well represent these elements…red for fire, blue (literally in Greek the color of hyacinth) for smoke, and yellow for sulfur or brimstone.

Is that a conclusive reason for the colors?

No, we don't know for sure, but God does have a reason for the color description being included and it may be to represent the fire, smoke, and sulfur.

The mounts of these riders are called horses, but they are not like any animals we have ever encountered. They have heads like lions which can breathe fire, smoke, and sulfur. What is exhaled out of them is deadly and able to kill the masses, one third of the world's population. But their tails are weapons as well. Their tails have heads, like snakes, and they inflict injury. These riders are loosed upon the earth, and they maim and kill.

The book of Revelation has been given to us as a sweet blessing, but also as a warning. It warns of the devastation that is to come, but God gave this vision almost 2000 years ago so that people could heed it's warning and prepare ahead of time. The things written about in this chapter, the horrible locusts and these mounted riders, are on the horizon and will all come to pass exactly as God has said.

But today there is yet time to call out to the Lord for salvation or to make any changes in our lives. And that is indeed such a sweet blessing.

But I have heard people say that if decisions for Christ can be made during the tribulation, then why not just wait until then to accept the Lord.

Let's examine why waiting is NOT a good choice.

First, we have no assurance of our next breath. People leave this earth with no time to think, let alone make decisions. Heart attacks, accidents, strokes, falls, allergic reactions, and almost instantly a person's breathing stops. Eternity is a long time to regret having put off the decision to know the Lord.

Second, when the rapture takes place, there is going to be mass chaos and destruction. People will suddenly be gone and whatever they were doing will be left unattended. Planes will be left with no pilots and eventually they will fall from the air. Driverless cars on cruise control will continue to move until they hit something and possibly explode. A pan on a stove will continue to cook until its contents burn and catch on fire. As the kitchen fire grows, gas lines will be ignited which will in turn ignite other gas lines. Surgeries will stop because the doctors, nurses, or anesthesiologist will instantly be gone. Vital programming of equipment will cease because the programmer will no longer be there. And this will happen all over the world. Accidents, fires, crashes will happen. Believers will be gone, but some who are not believers will die in the chaos.

Third, right now we have access to churches, and we know people who are Christians who are praying for nonbelievers to be saved. The Holy Spirit dwells in each believer. The presence of the Holy Spirit and the prayers of Christ followers today are still here. But when ALL Christians are taken off this planet, there will be a void. If a person will not accept Christ now, why would we think that they will when all of that is gone?

Waiting to come to Christ is a huge risk. Hearts get harder and harder until the result is evidenced. *Revelation 9:20-21 "The rest of mankind who were not killed by these plagues still did not repent of the work of their hands; they did not stop worshiping demons, and idols of gold, silver, bronze, stone and wood—idols that cannot see or hear or walk. Nor did they repent of their murders, their magic arts, their sexual immorality or their thefts."*

The more times someone rejects the Lord, the easier it becomes to reject the Lord.

REVELATION

CHAPTER 10

DAY 50

I absolutely love summer thunderstorms. Okay, maybe not at night when I'm trying to sleep, but during the heat of the day, they suddenly cool everything down a bit. That's nothing but refreshing. The lightening cracks, then the thunder sounds, I love it. But I have never heard the thunder speak.

"Then I saw another mighty angel coming down from heaven. He was robed in a cloud, with a rainbow above his head; his face was like the sun, and his legs were like fiery pillars. He was holding a little scroll, which lay open in his hand. He planted his right foot on the sea and his left foot on the land, and he gave a loud shout like the roar of a lion. When he shouted, the voices of the seven thunders spoke. And when the seven thunders spoke, I was about to write; but I heard a voice from heaven say, 'Seal up what the seven thunders have said and do not write it down.'" Revelation 10:1-4

Lest we forget the sheer enormous size of angels, here we are given an impressive picture of one. He is clothed in a robe made of the clouds. A rainbow encircles his head. His face is shining like the sun. His legs are like pillars of fire. He stands with one foot on the sea and one foot on the land. His voice is like the roar of a lion. It all says that so much of what we will see and experience in the presence of God will be mighty and immense and overwhelming and incredibly amazing.

It ignites a deep longing inside of me.

And the angel shouted, and when he shouted, seven thunders spoke. They had a message. John was ready to write it down. But a voice, bigger than the voice of the angel, commanded that this message be sealed up, stored away, and saved for a future time.

Does that make anyone else curious to first hear what thunder sounds like when it speaks, and secondly to know exactly what it was that the seven thunders spoke?

And yet, it wasn't to be revealed to us. Why?

I suppose for many reasons and of course we can only speculate, but one reason may be that this is too big for us to know ahead of time.

But it also tells us that we don't need to know everything about what will happen in the future. Some of it will be unsealed later. It is enough for us to know that God knows every second of every day and He is absolutely and reliably in charge of it all.

"Then the angel I had seen standing on the sea and on the land raised his right hand to heaven. And he swore by him who lives forever and ever, who created the heavens and all that is in them, the earth and all that is in it, and the sea and all that is in it, and said, 'There will be no more delay! But in the days when the seventh angel is about to sound his trumpet, the mystery of God will be accomplished, just as he announced to his servants the prophets.'" Revelation 10:5-7

John was given this glimpse of the future. In the vision, he saw an angel, a heavenly messenger, who comes to earth and stands between the land and the sea. He has a critically important message, and he backs it up with the greatest authority in the entire universe. This angel swore by the One who made the heavens, the earth, the sea, everything there is, everything we can see, touch, taste, smell, or hear. This message is from Almighty God. And this is it, *"There will be no more delay."*

Since Jesus left the earth, people have longed for, wondered, and speculated about His imminent return. Throughout history, people have declared that they had inside information, set dates, scared people, and it hasn't happened. God has been so incredibly patient with us humans. He has graciously allowed these last 2000 years for all of us to come to know Him. If He had returned in the 1800's we wouldn't have been born; we wouldn't have a place in eternity, and neither would our children or grandchildren. How grateful I am for His patience and that He waited for us.

But there is coming a day when God will say, enough is enough. *"There will be no more delay."*

How soon will that happen? How imminent is that moment? None of us knows that date. We simply know it will happen. This angel's message has all the authority of the Creator of the heavens, the earth, the sea, and everything in them. We can take it to the bank.

So, the take-away for us?

Be ready NOW!

DAY 51

Don't you just love a good mystery? I do. I thoroughly enjoy the "whodunit" detective story. I like it when I try to guess halfway into a book or movie, who the culprit is and speculate on their motives. The desire to know keeps me turning the page.

God knows that we love mysteries, so He has many in store for us. There were mysteries in the Old Testament that we have had the privilege of seeing revealed in Christ, in Israel, in prophecies unveiled in our lifetimes. It's exciting. It's amazing. It's faith building. God wants us to have eyes to see.

And right here in chapter 10 of Revelation, God informs us that one of the mysteries that had been spoken by the prophets is now going to be accomplished.

"But in the days when the seventh angel is about to sound his trumpet, the mystery of God will be accomplished, just as he announced to his servants the prophets." Revelation 10:7

And what is this mystery? Revelation 11:15 tells us when the seventh angel sounds his trumpet, loud voices in heaven begin to shout that God's rule will be established and His reign will be forever.

What a glorious revelation. The victory belongs to our Lord, so the victory belongs to us.

Our God reigns.

When life seems challenging, remember, He reigns.

When circumstances appear overwhelming, remember, His Kingdom will be established.

When darkness threatens to overtake us, remember, we win because He wins.

Hallelujah!

"Then the voice that I had heard from heaven spoke to me once more: 'Go, take the scroll that lies open in the hand of the angel who is standing on the sea and on the land.' So I went to the angel and asked him to give me the little scroll. He said to me, 'Take it and eat it. It will turn your stomach sour, but in your mouth it will be as sweet as honey.' I took the little scroll from the angel's hand and ate it. It tasted as sweet as honey in my mouth, but when I had eaten it, my stomach turned sour. Then I was told, 'You must prophesy again about many peoples, nations, languages and kings.'" Revelation 10:8-11

This angel, who was standing on the land and sea, had a scroll in his hand from God. John was told to eat the scroll. Okay, eating a scroll sounds like a pretty strange order. Here again we must go on the treasure hunt to see if we can discover anything about this request.

And, yes, we can. In the book of Ezekiel chapters 2 and 3, the prophet Ezekiel was given the same order. The Lord told him to eat a scroll that was held out to him. And when he ate it, it tasted sweet like honey. Then Ezekiel was told to go and prophesy to the people of Israel with these instructions, *"And whether they listen or fail to listen—for they are a rebellious people—they will know that a prophet has been among them." Ezekiel 2:5*

God was warning His people to turn from wickedness and yield their obstinate hearts to Him. God was graciously giving Ezekiel's generation time to repent. But God told Ezekiel that it was his job to feast on the Word, deliver the message, and be the messenger. The repentance was up to each person individually.

John was also told to devour these Words from God. They tasted sweet to him because He knew the Lord. He followed God. But telling people whose hearts are hardened is a challenge and upsetting to the stomach. And yet the job for John was to deliver the message, the results are for each one individually. Every person must choose.

It is the same for us. The Word of God tastes sweet for those whose hearts are tender and yielded to the Lord. His Word is delicious, like honey dripping from the comb, for those who know and love Him. But when we deliver a message that says judgment is coming, our hearts and stomachs may also very much react. But our job is the same as Ezekiel's and John's. We are called to feast on the Word. We are called to be the messengers. But then we also must remember that whether people listen or fail to listen, they have been told.

REVELATION

CHAPTER 11

DAY 52

When my husband and I moved to our house, there was a lovely green field right behind us. Every so often, a deer would show up to graze and play. I loved that. But then, one day surveyors showed up. They had their measuring rods, and I knew what it meant; my bucolic field was about to become a building project. And I couldn't do a thing about it because I didn't own the property. The owner has the right to do what he wants.

Well, in chapter 11 of Revelation, God sends John to do a bit of surveying himself.

"I was given a reed like a measuring rod and was told, 'Go and measure the temple of God and the altar, with its worshipers. But exclude the outer court; do not measure it, because it has been given to the Gentiles. They will trample on the holy city for 42 months.'" Revelation 11:1-2

These verses talk about a Temple that will be in Jerusalem as these prophecies unfold. As I am writing this, there is no Temple in Jerusalem.

But there will be.

How do I know? God's Word proclaims that it will be there. It is clear even from these verses that the Temple hosts some of the major events as the last seven years take place. God's Word is enough to trust that it will be there and for centuries that was all Christians could stand upon.

But not today, today we have even more evidence. Throughout Israel it has become the major mission of some significant teachers, leaders, political figures to determine how and when this Temple should be constructed.

The Temple Mount Faithful was established in 1967 and the Temple Institute was founded in 1987, both with the vision and mission to see the Temple constructed.

Musical instruments, priests' clothing, all the objects used for worship, and training for the priests have been or are being set in motion so that the Temple could be functioning within a very short time of the clearance being given for the go ahead.

A decade ago, we visited the Temple Institute and asked our guide how long it would take to construct the Temple once the way was given to begin. Her answer then astounded us. She said it would take less than a week.

How will this take place?

John was told by the Lord to go and measure the Temple area. This clearly indicates who owns this property. Governments may claim it. People may occupy it. But God clearly owns it because He is the One directing that it be surveyed. It is His to measure. It is His to build upon. There will be a Temple built on this spot. Again, how will this happen?

I don't know. I simply know it will. Could the word be given to begin construction today? It could. Could it be weeks or months? Very possibly. Within our lifetime? We'd like to think so.

It will happen. There will be a Temple in Jerusalem. God said it will be there, so it will be there.

The Lord has all of this under control.

God foretold it.

Our faith will become sight.

Keep looking.

And there is a reason this is so important. At some point during this seven-year tribulation time, two witnesses show up to teach, preach, prophecy, and do miracles.

God has outlined the principle of two witnesses throughout Scripture to help people to understand the validity of His message. It is what we see in these next verses.

"'And I will appoint my two witnesses, and they will prophesy for 1,260 days, clothed in sackcloth.' They are 'the two olive trees' and the two lampstands, and 'they stand before the Lord of the earth.'" Revelation 11:3-4

These two witnesses are not dressed for success. They have no fancy attire or perfect platform. They are standing on the Temple Mount dressed in sackcloth. It was a cloth made of goat's or camel's hair. It was the attire of some prophets and could represent complete brokenness or loss. It was what you would wear in great despair.

These two witnesses will both convey the same call. They will stand before the Lord even as they stand before the men and women of earth urging repentance. All of the earth will have their eyes on them, but most will not listen to them.

Even today, a video camera is on play at the Western Wall of the Temple Mount. You can see what is happening at the place where the message of these two men might well go out. The technology is already in place to broadcast these two witnesses proclaiming God's message for the nations.

Their word will be prophetic and life changing, and ultimately eternity changing for all who will respond. But tragically, for many it will fall on deaf ears. Some it will outrage, and they will make it their mission to bring these two voices to silence.

No one, nothing will be able to still their voices until the Lord declares that their mission is complete.

That is true for us also. When we are on the job for Him, He declares when we are finished. His work will go on, no matter what.

So, we must ask ourselves what our mission is for today.

Lord, who do I need to pray for? What do I need to do? Who can I help? Who needs encouragement? Will there be someone cross my path today who needs to hear the Gospel?

These two witnesses will be at exactly the right place at the exact right time, with the exact right message for exactly 1,260 days.

Let's make it our prayer to be at the right place at the right time with the message for as long as the Lord gives us.

DAY 53

As we read Revelation, we must remember that what we are reading is prophetic.

"If anyone tries to harm them, fire comes from their mouths and devours their enemies. This is how anyone who wants to harm them must die. They have power to shut up the heavens so that it will not rain during the time they are prophesying; and they have power to turn the waters into blood and to strike the earth with every kind of plague as often as they want." Revelation 11:5-6

No one, nothing will stop these two witnesses from sharing the truth of God's Word with a watching world. There will be those who try, but they will not be successful. They have fire that will come from their mouths, and the enemies will be stopped. Death will come to anyone who tries to harm them. The message will go out. My guess is that this will be the top of the evening news, the morning news, and everything in-between. Around the world, what God is doing will be proclaimed.

We see a hint of that happening today. Our news is often filled with killings, protests, riots, what we can do, what we can't do, what we can say, what we can't say. It's a challenging time. But God is still in the midst of all of it and using even the hard things. He is at work today. His Word is going out. He will be at work in the seven last years, using these two witnesses.

But the question is asked, "Who are these two witnesses?"

And that is such a good question. And even though we cannot be definitive, there are a few hints as to who they might be.

Let's start with what we do know about them.

They are witnesses. Their mission is to proclaim truth. And they will, without fear or compromise. They will not worry that the message offends or disturbs. There isn't time to be concerned about that. People will hear and either repent or reject.

They aren't worried about how they appear. They are dressed in sackcloth and their only concern is the message. They won't wait for touch-up make-up as the TV cameras show up. They will preach and keep preaching no matter what.

Their time will be limited. Every word counts. They probably won't waste time on small talk.

Weather forecasts won't be any concern because they will have the ability to shut up the heavens so it will not rain. Their preaching will not get rained out.

They are two olive trees and two lampstands. (Zechariah 4) Olive oil was used for healing, light, and food. Lampstands were the means to bring light into a place. These two witnesses are there to bring light, spiritual food, and healing to any who will listen.

Nothing or no one will be able to stop them until their mission is complete. Fire comes from their mouths, and enemies who try to stop them are struck down. The preaching continues.

They speak with the same God-ordained authority as Moses and Elijah. And just like Moses and Elijah, these two witnesses will bring down fire, and the water will be turned to blood.

So, is that the identity of these two?

It's a possibility. We know that Moses and Elijah appeared with Jesus on the Mount of Transfiguration before His crucifixion. Could they be the ones who will come before His final return?

Yes.

Could they be Enoch and Elijah? There are those who believe they will bring the witness because they did not yet experience a first death. So, could these two witnesses be Enoch and Elijah?

Yes.

Could they be two others who come for this final season of global preaching? The entire world will have the opportunity to tune in to hear the message of repentance and salvation. Could they be unknown until that time?

Yes.

Their identity will be revealed at exactly the right moment.

Their message is already revealed. Repent and come to Jesus. It will be the message then. It is the message now.

DAY 54

"*Now when they have finished their testimony, the beast that comes up from the Abyss will attack them, and overpower and kill them.*" *Revelation 11:7*

There is a glorious word imbedded into this verse. It is a word I long for in my walk here with the Lord. Do you see it?

It is the word finished.

These two witnesses will have completed their task. They will have done the job they were called to do. For exactly 1,260 days, they will have given their testimony.

How much will they sleep?

How often will they take a break?

Do they simply eat a few bites for strength to go back to it?

We aren't given those details. We don't really need to know that at this moment. We do know that they will have done the job they were put on earth to do and then they will be finished.

They will do their job and do it well.

Will everyone embrace their message?

No, they will not.

Many will be infuriated by what these two witnesses have to say. But that won't stop them from sharing truth until their time is over. It is only then that the enemy will have the power to overtake them. It is only then that the beast can overpower them and take their lives.

But they will finish, and when they are done, it will be okay to give their lives. It will be for us also.

We grieve over death here, but the truth is that for us who know and follow Jesus, it is simply a portal. It is the gateway into our real life.

These two witnesses give everything, and then their voices are silenced, but their ministry is not. The Gospel is so powerful that even death cannot silence its content.

"Their bodies will lie in the public square of the great city—which is figuratively called Sodom and Egypt—where also their Lord was crucified. For three and a half days some from every people, tribe, language and nation will gaze on their bodies and refuse them burial. The inhabitants of the earth will gloat over them and will celebrate by sending each other gifts, because these two prophets had tormented those who live on the earth." Revelation 11:8-10

People will take great delight in the death of these two prophets, viewing it as a victory. After three and a half years of listening to these voices, finally the world will rejoice at their silence.

That is the heartbreak for those who reject the truth. Joy is found in what brings death.

Celebrations come because they think truth is silenced.

But what we must remember is that this kind of rejoicing is short lived. The world thinks they are rid of the truth. But truth never dies. Jesus Christ is the way, the truth, and the life. He was crucified and those who stood by thought it was over. But truth cannot be silenced. Truth will rise.

The world will watch in terror as these international events unfold. People from around the globe, watching the latest news of the deaths of the two witnesses, will be gloating and rejoicing at their deaths.

But then suddenly, those two who were dead come back to life.

"But after the three and a half days the breath of life from God entered them, and they stood on their feet, and terror struck those who saw them. Then they heard a loud voice from heaven saying to them, 'Come up here.' And they went up to heaven in a cloud, while their enemies looked on." Revelation 11:11-12

This event unfolds unlike any those watching have ever seen. Most will have no clue as to what is happening. This international audience, gazing on the dead bodies of God's witnesses, suddenly witness these two dead men beginning to breathe. Dead for three and a half days, reminiscent of their preaching for three and a half years, these two provide living proof of God's resurrection power. The world has been smirking, cheering, rejoicing because they've been looking at their dead bodies, certain they had the victory. But we must remember that God always has the last word. He breathes life into these two men, and they stand to their feet. The world sees the dead rise before their very eyes. They literally witness dead men walking.

Then God pronounces to them, *"Come up here."* And these two are caught up to heaven in a cloud. What an incredible event to witness. Bigger than any election, coronation, space lift-off, this will be greater than anything ever witnessed by this crowd.

These two were dead but then suddenly alive in a moment.

Miraculous!

But every bit as miraculous is an event that takes lives from death to life every day. It is inviting Christ to forgive us of our sins and asking Him to come into our lives. In our sin, we are headed to death and agony. When we repent and invite Christ into our lives, suddenly we are on a path to eternal life. In a matter of moments, we go from eternal death to eternal life.

Miraculous!

DAY 55

If someone puts on the brakes a little too fast...if I see one of the grandkids start to fall...if my hands are too full and something starts to slip...my response? Woe, woe, woe! Yes, those three woes just automatically come from my lips. It's a warning to me or someone else to watch out.

In these end days we have three woes, certainly more severe than anything we've ever experienced, but still a warning, coming down upon the world.

"At that very hour there was a severe earthquake and a tenth of the city collapsed. Seven thousand people were killed in the earthquake, and the survivors were terrified and gave glory to the God of heaven. The second woe has passed; the third woe is coming soon." Revelation 11:13-14

An earthquake will erupt from the belly of the earth. We already know the death count. It is recorded before it ever happens. The news will announce that seven thousand have died. It is future but the count is as set in stone as if it were past. God knows what has happened, what is happening, what will happen.

This is one of the proofs positive that God's Word is true. The future has been written in advance.

This earthquake claims seven thousand lives.

Terrified survivors will recognize the fact that God is ultimately in charge.

What does it take for us? Do we respond daily, giving glory to God and thanking Him for what He is doing, or do we have to wait until tragedy strikes?

The Lord wants our love and devotion every hour of every day, good times, bad times, every time in between.

One of the intriguing things about the book of Revelation is that often it's as though we are watching a split screen TV. We see what is happening on the earth, but then what is happening in the heavenlies. It's a sweet reminder that God is in charge.

"The seventh angel sounded his trumpet, and there were loud voices in heaven, which said: 'The kingdom of the world has become the kingdom of our Lord and of his Messiah, and he will reign for ever and ever.'" Revelation 11:15

While there is chaos on the earth, there is worship in heaven.

History is rampant with the stories of those who have tried to build kingdoms for themselves. It has happened through negotiations, treaties, wars, slavery, destruction, greed, hatred, agreements, disagreements, marriages, covenants, terrorism, handshakes, assassinations. But here is the conclusion, no matter what the means, scope, heart behind any of these attempts at kingdom building, they have one thing in common. They have all failed. Not one earthly kingdom will stand.

One day it will all come back to where it was always supposed to be, one Kingdom, the Kingdom of the Lord Jesus Christ. It is present today and all who trust and follow Christ are in that Kingdom. But there is soon coming a time when His Kingdom will fill the earth. Announced by a loud voice from heaven, He will reign for ever and ever.

It is nearer today than any other time.

"And the twenty-four elders, who were seated on their thrones before God, fell on their faces and worshiped God, saying: 'We give thanks to you, Lord God Almighty, the One who is and who was, because you have taken your great power and have begun to reign. The nations were angry, and your wrath has come. The time has come for judging the dead, and for rewarding your servants the prophets and your people who revere your name, both great and small—and for destroying those who destroy the earth.'" Revelation 11:16-18

In these few verses, we are shown one of the most humble positions we can ever take. These twenty-four elders fall on their faces and worship God. They are facedown. But keep in mind that the lowest we can be, becomes one of the most powerful places we can be. These elders begin to worship. Heaven is filled with their praise and testimony of what God is doing. It is powerful.

God's plan for the earth will be accomplished. No rhetoric, pandemic, destruction, planning, conniving, warring can stop what God is doing right now and what He will do. His work cannot be stopped.

"Then God's temple in heaven was opened, and within his temple was seen the ark of his covenant. And there came flashes of lightning, rumblings, peals of thunder, an earthquake and a severe hailstorm." Revelation 11:19

There is much speculation as to the location of the Ark of the Covenant. It has been the subject of movies, documentaries, articles, searches.

But where is it today?

We don't know.

What we do know from this passage in Revelation is that there is an Ark of the Covenant in heaven, and it is the original. The one that became famous here on earth was modeled after the heavenly one. God instructed Moses exactly how to build it.

Everything God gave to the Children of Israel to be used in their worship had a purpose. It was all to point to our relationship with the Lord.

During the tribulation, the Temple will once again stand as a testimony to who the Lord is and how He wants to dwell in the hearts and lives of people. There will be some who see and respond, and there will be some who reject the Truth.

It is the same today. The testimony of God's love and desire to live in us is all around us. We must choose. Do we accept and follow Him or reject and go our own way?

It is up to us.

REVELATION
CHAPTER 12

DAY 56

I've taught English and with that I taught writing. Not all my students loved writing assignments. In fact, most of them didn't. Maybe one of the reasons for that is because there are lots of rules. Another reason might have been some of the language they had to know. Similes, metaphors, hyperbole, allegory, even humor to name a few. Most of the time they were okay with the humor one, but I wanted them to understand that using some of the literary devices could make their writing more interesting, more powerful.

The Bible is the most powerful book ever written and most of it is to be taken literally. But it also uses imagery, and we see some of that in Revelation. Chapter 12 begins by using metaphors to point to an event.

Revelation 12:1-2, "A great sign appeared in heaven: a woman clothed with the sun, with the moon under her feet and a crown of twelve stars on her head. She was pregnant and cried out in pain as she was about to give birth."

What is this event that's being referenced?

It's the birth of Christ.

In this passage, the woman that is being referred to is Israel. Way back in the covenant to Abraham, previously named Abram, God told him that he would be the father of a nation.

Genesis 12:1-3, "The Lord had said to Abram, 'Go from your country, your people and your father's household to the land I will show you. I will make you into a great nation, and I will bless you; I will make your name great, and you will be a blessing. I will bless those who bless you, and whoever curses you I will curse; and all peoples on earth will be blessed through you.'"

Abraham became the father of Isaac. Isaac became the father of Jacob. Jacob became the father of twelve sons who became the patriarchs of the nation of Israel. These are the twelve stars that are being referred to in these Revelation verses. I love that often Scripture interprets Scripture. We see the reference of stars, moon, and sun in Genesis 37 as Joseph recounted his second dream. *"Listen,' he said, 'I had another dream, and this time the sun and moon and eleven stars were bowing down to me.'"*

Joseph, as one of the sons, made the twelfth star that is spoken of in Revelation.

These heavenly bodies, the stars, the sun, and moon in Revelation, are a reference to the nation of Israel. It was through Israel that a very special birth took place. The pain spoken of here is an abundance of tribulations and trials: slavery, captivity, wandering in the wilderness, persecution down through the ages for Israel. But then at just the right moment an angel appeared to a young Jewish virgin to give the best news the world would ever receive. She would give birth to the long awaited One, the Messiah.

DAY 57

Revelation 12:3, "Then another sign appeared in heaven: an enormous red dragon with seven heads and ten horns and seven crowns on its heads."

An enormous red dragon…sounds like something from a fairy tale, doesn't it? But this is no children's story. We see a similar image in Daniel chapter 7. It is found in his vision of things that are to come. This dragon is real and Revelation 12:9 tells us who it is. It is Satan, the devil. The seven heads, seven crowns, and ten horns all represent kingdoms that follow this evil one during the end times. The world will grow increasingly wicked and will submit to the devil's leadership. Things will go from bad, to very bad, to worse.

Let's think back over our own lifetimes. Are things better or worse today than they were when we were kids? I remember a day when keys could be left in cars, doors were unlocked… even at night. Identity theft was not a term we had ever heard. Stranger danger was not prevalent and a person's handshake or their word was enough to seal a deal.

Not so today. The closer we get to the end, the more callous, hardened, and evil the world gets. Rioting, looting, anarchy have all been seen over the last weeks, months, and years. Stealing, killing, and destruction are the devil's wheelhouse. The world is setting up for Satan to make his big move. He will use a charismatic world leader to easily entice and convince people that a global plan for peace, security, safety is imperative. The devil will also be behind the actions of world leaders to sway people to follow.

Here in Revelation 12, we see the picture of the birth of Christ, the Messiah, through the nation of Israel, and the image of the dragon, Satan, who was waiting, watching, ready.

In the Garden of Eden, Satan came as a serpent. After he enticed Adam and Eve to sin, God told the serpent he would crawl on the ground, eat dust, and have his head crushed by the Seed of the woman. Since that time the devil's goal has been to wipe out the nation of people through whom that Seed, Jesus, would come. If he could destroy the nation, he could prevent the birth and that would negate God's plan of redemption. That nation was Israel. And the devil hates Israel, God's chosen people.

But since Jesus came, the devil's plan has escalated and he is now not only bent on destroying Israel, but Christians as well.

Evil is growing in our world, but once again, we as believers can be encouraged. Jesus will never forsake us. He is with us every day through every trial, every hardship. Remember, *"You, dear children, are from God and have overcome them, because the one who is in you is greater than the one who is in the world." 1 John 4:4*

Satan is the dragon who desired to destroy God's plan. *Its tail swept a third of the stars out of the sky and flung them to the earth. The dragon stood in front of the woman who was about to give birth, so that it might devour her child the moment he was born." Revelation 12:4*

The woman represents Israel. The red dragon is the devil, the evil one who tried to overthrow heaven, but he, along with one third of the angels, was cast out. This means that thousands, perhaps millions of demonic angels followed him. At that moment, the devil suffered a terrible blow and since that time, he has sought to overtake heaven. If he could subvert the plan of God, he might have a chance. He worked to try to destroy the nation of Israel through wars, wicked kings, disobedience, slavery, plots to kill them, and when that didn't work, he attempted to kill Jesus right from the outset.

The one he used for the attempted murder was Herod. Magi came to Jerusalem following the sign they had seen in the heavens. It was the star that led them. When they arrived in Jerusalem, they asked, *"...Where is the one who has been born king of the Jews? We saw his star when it rose and have come to worship him."* Matthew 2:2

Herod was upset. He was the king of the Jews or at least that's what he thought. His anger rose and a plot swirled inside him, but he didn't allow the wise men to see. He feigned a desire to worship the new King. But he had no plans for worship, his plan was to kill the One the wise men called the King.

The magi followed God's sign. They encountered the true King of the Jews and then, being warned in a dream, left by a different way. After the wise men did not return, Herod cast a wide net to accomplish his death plot. He ordered all the baby boys from the vicinity of Bethlehem, who were two years old and younger, killed. But God had Joseph take Mary and baby Jesus to Egypt and away from Herod. Satan had stood ready to destroy the One who came to be the Savior of the World, but Jesus was protected. The devil's plan for the killing of Jesus was foiled.

God's plan has always been fulfilled.

God's plan will always be fulfilled.

DAY 58

Let's remember who the woman in chapter 12 is. She represents Israel.

"She gave birth to a son, a male child, who 'will rule all the nations with an iron scepter.' And her child was snatched up to God and to his throne." Revelation 12:5

An iron scepter is a phrase used here. It is referred to as well in Revelation 2 and 19, and in Psalm 2. A scepter indicates someone who rules. Kings have scepters. An iron scepter represents a power that is unyielding. There is no debate, no argument. Jesus has absolute control. This rule was prophesied long ago.

In Genesis, when Jacob was about to die, he called in his twelve sons and spoke prophecies over them. The fourth son, Judah, was brought before his father and Jacob gave this prophecy, *"The scepter will not depart from Judah, nor the ruler's staff from between his feet, until he to whom it belongs shall come and the obedience of the nations shall be his." Genesis 49:10*

Jacob told Judah that it would be through his line that kings would come. But it also indicated that THE KING, the ultimate King of all Kings, would come who would rule forever.

That One is Jesus.

When Jesus came the first time, He came as the Lamb of God. He came to be the sin sacrifice for the world. The first time He came as a Lamb, but the Messiah has also been referred to as the Lion of Judah. Jesus is coming again and this time to rule and reign. When it says an iron scepter, it indicates that

ALL authority and ALL power will be held by the Messiah, over ALL governments. He will rule and He will do it forever.

Isaiah also prophesied this, hundreds of years before. *"For to us a child is born, to us a son is given, and the government will be on his shoulders. And he will be called Wonderful Counselor, Mighty God, Everlasting Father, Prince of Peace. Of the greatness of his government and peace there will be no end. He will reign on David's throne and over his kingdom, establishing and upholding it with justice and righteousness from that time on and forever. The zeal of the Lord Almighty will accomplish this."* Isaiah 9:6-7

Jesus is the King of Kings.

Right now, our Lord is seated on the throne in heaven, but He will not stay there. He is coming. He will set up His Kingdom here. And He is going to rule with an iron scepter from that time on and forever.

"The woman fled into the wilderness to a place prepared for her by God, where she might be taken care of for 1,260 days." Revelation 12:6

In this verse we are once again referring to Israel, the woman who will need to flee. The nation of Israel has been persecuted down through the ages.

In Exodus, the Jewish people were exiled, enslaved, tortured, and killed. Through it all they longed for a deliverer. Then Moses came and led them out of bondage from Egypt.

Centuries later they were in bondage under Roman rule and longed for a deliverer. One did come, but many missed Him. The people were looking for a military leader who would overthrow the Roman government and establish His Kingdom for Israel.

Jesus did come as a Deliverer but not to free them from the bondage of Rome.

He came to free the world from the bondage of sin. That was so much greater, so much better. But because Jesus came the first time as a Lamb and not a Lion, many refused to see. The world could have known. Hundreds of prophecies were given. Genesis 22, Isaiah 53, and Psalm 22 are pictures of what was to come, and that the Messiah would first have to suffer and die.

But because He did not come the way people wanted, many rejected Him.

During the tribulation period, many of the Children of Israel will have their eyes opened. Then they will see. They will understand that Jesus was and is the long-awaited Messiah. The book of Revelation shows us God's plan for redemption. In Revelation 12:6, we see that many Jews will flee into the wilderness. God has prepared a place for them to run to for safety. Biblical scholars believe this place may be Petra. There are caves and places to hide.

Daniel 11:41 indicates that some places in the Middle East will be protected by God and the antichrist will not be able to wreak havoc there.

For three and a half years, 1260 days on the Jewish calendar, many Jewish believers will have a place to run to and they will take refuge.

God will protect and guard them.

DAY 59

I've been to parades. As I watch, I have a lovely view of what's directly in front of me, floats, marching bands, horses with their riders, any number of parade worthy displays. I can also see a little forward to where the floats are headed, and as I stare back, I can see some of the next displays. But that's about it. I cannot see the end and the beginning of the parade at the same time. I see only what's in front of me and it by no means encompasses the whole procession.

But God has a completely different view.

We need to remember that God is outside of time and space. He sees the whole parade. He sees all of life, all of time, all the events, the beginning, the end, and everything in-between. Neither His timetable nor His view is the same as ours. He sees the end from the beginning.

Often, when we read the Bible, it lists chronological events, but not always. Sometimes things are out of sequence. There could be future events or past events referenced.

Also, passages can be multilayered. A portion of Scripture could be giving us some historical event. As we read the same passage, we might realize that it is as current as today's news in how it applies to our lives. But it might also hold a prophecy and show something that is yet to come. And that makes a lot of sense. Jesus is the Word made flesh. In Revelation 1, it tells us that He is *"the One who is, and who was, and who is to come, the Almighty."* We can rest in knowing that God's beautiful Word often has layers of meaning. It's part of the treasure hunt as we dig deeper into each verse.

Here in Revelation 12, we have a reference to a past event, a long past event, before human history past event. *"Then war broke out in heaven. Michael and his angels fought against the dragon, and the dragon and his angels fought back. But he was not strong enough, and they lost their place in heaven. The great dragon was hurled down—that ancient serpent called the devil, or Satan, who leads the whole world astray. He was hurled to the earth, and his angels with him."* Revelation 12:7-9

We don't know when, but some time long ago before Adam and Eve were created, the devil tried to usurp God's authority.

Pride entered the one referred to as Lucifer.

Pride caused him to believe that he could become like God.

Pride led him to believe he could overthrow heaven.

And that same pride helped him deceive one third of all the angels into following him.

Then war broke out, but the archangel Michael and the other two thirds of the angels defeated Satan and his horde. The devil was not strong enough to defeat God's angelic army. The result? Satan and his followers were exiled from God's Kingdom. We read about that in Isaiah 14 and Ezekiel 28.

It began with pride. That may be the beginning place for most sin. Pride played a huge part when sin began with mankind. In the Garden of Eden, Satan came with a question, *"Did God really say?"* He was trying to make Eve question and doubt what God said. And then as her head was wrapped around the question, he appealed to her pride, *"You will be like God."* That was the clincher. The fruit looked good, and it would make her wise. She ate and gave some to Adam who was with her. They both knew it was wrong. But the father of lies caused her to question and then he convinced her that she didn't really have to listen and obey what God said. Adam made that same choice.

It's a tactic Satan continues to use. His ploy? Convince people to believe that God's Word is archaic, or that it couldn't possibly all be true, or that it doesn't really mean what it says. Then the devil whispers something like, "You know what's best for your own life. You can make your own way. All roads lead to God. You can choose your own path."

This is what Jesus said: *"I am the way and the truth and the life. No one comes to the Father except through me." John 14:6*

There is only one way to eternal life.

This next passage from Revelation 12 continues with Satan's defeat and his being cast out of heaven.

"Then war broke out in heaven. Michael and his angels fought against the dragon, and the dragon and his angels fought back. But he was not strong enough, and they lost their place in heaven. The great dragon was hurled down—that ancient serpent called the devil, or Satan, who leads the whole world astray. He was hurled to the earth, and his angels with him. Then I heard a loud voice in heaven say: 'Now have come the salvation and the power and the kingdom of our God, and the authority of his Messiah. For the accuser of our brothers and sisters, who accuses them before our God day and night, has been hurled down.'" Revelation 12:7-9

Long ago in heaven, the devil was defeated. He was cast down. Unfortunately, though, he is still on a rampage here on earth to deceive as many as possible. Today he rants, rages, raves, and causes destruction. He is the tempter, the thief, the killer, the destroyer, and the accuser. He was defeated in heaven, but for us, right now, we must still deal with his attacks.

The Bible gives us plans for overcoming. We find one in *Ephesians 6:10-17, "Finally, be strong in the Lord and in his mighty power. Put on the full armor of God, so that you can take your stand against the devil's schemes. For our struggle is not against flesh and blood, but against the rulers, against the authorities, against the powers of this dark world and against the spiritual forces of evil in the heavenly realms. Therefore put on the full armor of God, so that when the day of evil comes, you may be able to stand your ground, and after you have done everything, to stand. Stand firm then, with the belt of truth buckled around your waist, with the breastplate of righteousness in place, and with your feet fitted with the readiness that comes from the gospel of peace. In addition to all this, take up the shield of faith, with which you can extinguish all the flaming arrows of the evil one. Take the helmet of salvation and the sword of the Spirit, which is the word of God."*

As we've discussed, the Word of God is multilayered. It covers events in the past, what is happening now, and events that are yet to occur. These Revelation verses fall into that same pattern of what was, what is, and what is to come.

What was...the devil was cast out of heaven.

What is...we have God's Word, His heavenly armor, that we can put on to fight against the evil one. We can defeat him. And then, having done all, we can stand!

What is to come...someday the devil will meet his final destination. We will read more about that later when we get to Revelation 20, when he will be cast down for good.

DAY 60

In this chapter, we begin with a passage from *2 Thessalonians 2:9-12*. *"The coming of the lawless one will be in accordance with how Satan works. He will use all sorts of displays of power through signs and wonders that serve the lie, and all the ways that wickedness deceives those who are perishing. They perish because they refused to love the truth and so be saved. For this reason God sends them a powerful delusion so that they will believe the lie and so that all will be condemned who have not believed the truth but have delighted in wickedness."*

As we've shared previously, the devil is working to defeat mankind. He uses deception, accusation, temptation, delusion.

As horrible as it is, people fall into his traps and believe the lies and eventually the ultimate lie that leads them to eternal death.

As Christ followers, we must be aware and on guard. Putting on the full armor of God is how we fight not only for ourselves, but also for our families and loved ones that they will not fall into the devil's traps. We pray for them.

Considering what we've read from 2 Thessalonians and having examined Ephesians 6, we're going to look at a three-tiered outline for overcoming the evil one, here in Revelation 12. *"Then I heard a loud voice in heaven say: Now have come the salvation and the power and the kingdom of our God, and the authority of his Messiah. For the accuser of our brothers and sisters, who accuses them before our God day and night, has been hurled down. They triumphed over him by the blood of the Lamb and by the word of their testimony; they did not love their lives so much as to shrink from death." Revelation 12:10-11*

Let's break this apart. First, it says they triumphed over the accuser, the devil, by the blood of the Lamb. There is no substance more powerful than this. The blood of Jesus was shed for our salvation, for our protection, for overcoming the devil. When we come to Christ, we are covered by His blood. We take on His sacrifice and get the free gift of salvation. We can claim that covering in any and every situation we encounter. The devil cowers at the blood of Jesus. He knows it is his defeat.

Secondly, they triumphed over the devil by the word of their testimony. This is so powerful. It is our story, how we came to know the Lord. For each of us, our testimony is unique, even if we share similar circumstances. Exactly how, when, and where we clearly heard, understood, and accepted the gift of salvation is singular to us. It's not debatable, because it's our story. It is such a powerful tool in our arsenal against the devil. When we are tempted to doubt, we can reference back to that time when we know that we asked Jesus to be our Lord and Savior.

And the third tier tells us that they triumphed over the devil by not loving their lives so much that they would shrink from death. His tactics are clear. He steals, kills, and destroys. His ultimate goal is to kill God's crowning creation, mankind, and to take as many as he can to join him for eternity. Fear of death is a ploy that Satan will use to make people cower. It has happened down through the ages. Persecutors have made people face death with the warning that if they wouldn't deny Christ they would be shot, face the sword, be thrown to wild beasts, drawn and quartered, or any number of cruel and terrible ways to die. They tried to make them deny the Savior. People have been, and still are today, faced with a decision: deny Christ and the persecutor will let them live, or stand for Christ and die. This threat still happens in places around the world.

But the threat is just that, a threat. In reality, the truth is just the opposite. Deny Christ and die, stand for Christ and live...eternally.

Our lives here are a mere nanosecond in light of eternity. They are a breath.

Physical death is not the worst thing. Denying Christ is.

How can we stand if we face persecution and are confronted with death?

Here's the answer: they overcame the devil by the blood of the Lamb, the word of their testimony, and they did not love their lives even when faced with death.

The devil has worked for millennia to put his evil plan in place. He is still working. But what he knows is that his days are numbered.

"Therefore rejoice, you heavens and you who dwell in them! But woe to the earth and the sea, because the devil has gone down to you! He is filled with fury, because he knows that his time is short." Revelation 12:12

The devil and his demonic horde were cast out of heaven. He tried to usurp God's authority. Pride made him believe he had the power to defeat the heavenly host. Satan fought, but when the battle was done, he was defeated and cast to the earth. Fury raged in him and since his defeat he has tried to wipe out God's creation. He has lied, stolen, deceived, tricked, and killed. He began with Adam and Eve. Oh, how he wanted them to succumb to his scheme. He conversed with Eve in the guise of a snake. He lied and sadly they did fall for his trickery. That might have been a glorious moment for the evil one, except that God in His amazing grace provided a plan. A Savior would come who would crush the head of the serpent.

A plan of redemption and salvation for all mankind was put into place. Then the liar, Satan, schemed again. He did his best to circumvent the coming of that One. He tried to wipe out the very nation through whom the Savior would come. The Israelites were enslaved for generations and then the baby boys were killed. If the boys were gone, the nation would cease to exist. But that plan failed because God miraculously saved Moses and sent him as the deliverer. The nation of Israel was set free. The devil may have believed he had the Israelites cornered with the Red Sea in front and Pharaoh's army bearing down. But God saved them right through the waters.

When the devil saw he could not destroy Israel, he thought he could kill the promised Savior. Herod had the baby boys killed in Bethlehem.

Multiple times the devil attempted to thwart God's plan as he tried to kill Jesus. Until finally at the cross, he may have dusted off his hands in a sign of victory. But the cross was not the end. It was God's amazing salvation plan, because Victory was coming, and the grave could not hold the resurrected Lord.

At every turn, Satan faced defeat. Now, with each new day, he knows his time grows shorter, but it also means his fury grows stronger. He is not yet finished. Today, he furiously plans yet another battle.

DAY 61

"*When the dragon saw that he had been hurled to the earth, he pursued the woman who had given birth to the male child. The woman was given the two wings of a great eagle, so that she might fly to the place prepared for her in the wilderness, where she would be taken care of for a time, times and half a time, out of the serpent's reach. Then from his mouth the serpent spewed water like a river, to overtake the woman and sweep her away with the torrent. But the earth helped the woman by opening its mouth and swallowing the river that the dragon had spewed out of his mouth.*" *Revelation 12:13-16*

Once again, let's review this symbolism. The dragon is the devil, so full of rage that his goal is annihilation of God's chosen people. The woman represents Israel, the nation through whom God's amazing plan of salvation has come. Jesus is the male child, the One promised way back in the Garden of Eden, who would crush the head of the serpent.

Years after the Garden of Eden, a promise came to Abraham that a nation would be birthed from his seed. Isaac was the son of that promise and then came Jacob, the second son of Isaac. He was born grabbing onto the foot of his twin, Esau. The two fought and rivaled. God renamed Jacob, calling him Israel, and he became the father of twelve sons. Those twelve sons became what we now refer to as the Twelve Tribes. Today their descendants are the nation of Israel.

From way back in the Garden, the devil schemed and fought against the promises of God. Destruction and death were his goal and that continues today. Israel is a most hated nation.

The tiny country is surrounded by people groups who want to wipe it off the map. Yet God's plan for Israel stands. He promised the land to Abraham's descendants and in 1948 Israel was declared a sovereign nation. So, the devil continues to fight and will continue even into the end times. The serpent will pursue and use any means possible to destroy Israel.

In this scene from Revelation, the evil one uses a flood. This may represent real waters coming in torrents, but it could also be symbolic of some other destruction that would come like a flood to wipe out the Israel remnant.

But God will supernaturally lift His chosen ones from the destruction onto the wings of an eagle to bring them to safety.

What is the eagle?

An airplane? Possibly.

An angel? We cannot know for sure.

What we do know is that there is protection and safety in His wings. *Isaiah 40:31, "…but those who hope in the Lord will renew their strength. They will soar on wings like eagles; they will run and not grow weary, they will walk and not be faint."*

The devil hates Israel. We've established that. One of the reasons for Satan's hatred is because Israel is the line through which the Messiah came. When God told the serpent that his head would be crushed by the Seed of the woman, the devil would have understood God's meaning…his days were numbered, and it would be Messiah who would destroy him.

As we see here in Revelation, time is even shorter for him now. So, his fury is increased. *"Then the dragon was enraged at the woman and went off to wage war against the rest of her offspring—those who keep God's commands and hold fast their testimony about Jesus." Revelation 12:17*

Yes, the devil hates Israel, but he also hates Christians. We are the fruit of the plan of God. Jesus came to die so we might live. Everywhere we go, every person we meet, every post we make on social media, every interaction we have are all opportunities to share Christ.

Christianity started with Jesus and a handful of followers. It was a small group. After the resurrection, there were about 120 who met together praying. Then 3000 more were added at Pentecost. And the message spread, and more believers were added.

The devil tried, oh yes, he tried to stamp it out. But every place his foot landed, it only spread the Good News further from Jerusalem to Judea, Samaria, and the uttermost parts of the world. The disciples were dynamos, and the rippling effect began.

Threats couldn't silence it.

Intimidation couldn't slow it.

Persecution couldn't crush it.

Death couldn't quell it.

The followers of Christ became evangelists. They knew the most important thing in life was to know Christ and to make Him known. Everything else paled by comparison.

So, what about us? Who can we tell? How can we share? It is the best news ever given that we can have our sins forgiven and we can be born into God's eternal family.

Revelation 12:12 tells us that the devil knows his time is short. But that also means time is winding down for us. Which day will be the last? Which opportunity will be our final chance to share God's amazing plan of salvation.

Will it be today?

Possibly tomorrow?

If you knew Jesus was coming back tomorrow, how would you spend today?

The disciples believed the return of Christ might be in their lifetime. They wasted no time.

With everything in me, I believe His return could be in our lifetime. Let's not waste time either.

God is calling every one of us who know Christ to be dynamos. Look around. Who can we tell? The world needs Jesus.

REVELATION

CHAPTER 13

DAY 62

When you go to a well-rehearsed play, you know that the stage is set, the actors are ready, the curtain lifts, and the action continues until the last word of the last scene is spoken. There are comedies, mysteries, action-packed dramas, and real nail-biters. And the book of Revelation can be put under several of those genres.

But this book also lets us know that everything is being prepared for the last scene here on earth. It doesn't have to be feared because repeatedly we see that this is God at work. We can trust Him that He has it all under His control.

There are three evil players on earth's stage for this seven-year end-time event called the tribulation. The first is the dragon who, as we saw from chapter 12, is Satan, the serpent. He has been constantly working throughout history with wicked plots and evil intent since he approached Eve in the Garden. He is a master of deception, and we must always remember that his native language is lies. Everything out of his mouth is laced with untruth, falsehood, and iniquity, which is a twisting of the truth. He takes a little bit of truth and twists it, so it sounds good, looks good, tastes good, but isn't good. We saw it in the Garden; we see it now. The Bible is very clear that Satan comes to steal, kill, and destroy.

Yes, Satan, the dragon, the serpent, is alive and thriving in our world today, but he will be vehemently working during the last seven years. *"The dragon stood on the shore of the sea. And I saw a beast coming out of the sea. It had ten horns and seven heads, with ten crowns on its horns, and on each head a blasphemous name." Revelation 13:1*

Verse 1 tells us that this dragon stands by the sea waiting for the appearance of the beast. The word sea could literally refer to the sea but could possibly mean a sea of people around the world.

Satan knows a lot. He has much power, but do not be deceived, he is not all-powerful or all-knowing. Only God has those attributes. Satan doesn't know God's timing. So, throughout history he has had a man ready and waiting to step onto the global stage. The pharaohs, many kings, Antiochus Epiphanes, the Caesars, Hitler, and some modern-day dictators would all love to claim the title of global leader. To date, none has been able to achieve that. But they have shared a common denominator. They have been evil.

But if we look back and think that they were evil vile characters, just wait for this final ruler's appearance. He will make those guys' actions look like child's play. Satan will endow this wicked person with demonic power.

This global leader has many names, antichrist, the beast, the man of intrigue, the man of lawlessness, to name a few. This beast will be the personification of evil.

So, the first player is Satan, the second is the beast or the antichrist. The term "anti" can mean against; it can also mean in place of. Both are true. This vile being will stand against our Lord and Savior, Jesus, demanding worship. Looking and acting like the savior the world wants and has been longing for, clamoring for, he will appear perfect and probably have solutions for the world's ills. Bringing peace and seeming too good to be true, he will look like the fulfillment of everything the world has waited for, and they will be deceived, bow down and worship the beast.

Then the third in this cast of evil characters is the false prophet. Notice the word false. His job will be to get everyone, small and great, to bow down and worship the beast. We will expand on his role more later.

So, Satan presents his fake messiah, his man for the job, and introduces his sidekick, the false prophet. These three stand and rule for seven years, a deceptive trio for the world.

God is a trinity, Father, Son, and Holy Spirit. Satan's attempt will be to imitate the Holy Trinity with this unholy trio, Satan, the antichrist, and the false prophet. The Bible tells us that many people will be deceived.

Pray for people's eyes to be opened to truth.

DAY 63

I was driving down the street and saw a billboard. It stated in big, bold, black letters, "Psychics Needed, Call!" Then underneath that message it read, "You know the number!" I laughed, because the real message behind the message was that if you really were a true psychic, able to see well into the future, something as simple as a phone number would be no problem to discern.

Throughout history there have been soothsayers, false prophets, mediums, those who have claimed to be able to predict the future. And there have been a few times when they have hit the nail on the head with a prediction here or there. To the world they have appeared impressive with their abilities and have produced a following. But the mark of a true prophet is nothing short of 100% accuracy. Anything else denotes a false prophet. With the Bible, what we see is that all of it is 100% correct. Every bit of it is true; every prophecy in it is accurate. When we read about future events, we can stake our lives on the fact that these things will take place.

"The dragon stood on the shore of the sea. And I saw a beast coming out of the sea. It had ten horns and seven heads, with ten crowns on its horns, and on each head a blasphemous name. The beast I saw resembled a leopard, but had feet like those of a bear and a mouth like that of a lion. The dragon gave the beast his power and his throne and great authority." Revelation 13:1-2

This beast is different from all other rulers who have reigned on earth. He is more of an amalgamation of evil than any being anyone has ever seen. He has ten horns. In Scripture horns represent power. So, ten means he wields a great deal of power. Possibly there are ten nations, or maybe ten global regions, that turn over their authority and rule to him.

Furthermore, he has seven heads and looks like a leopard, feet like a bear, with a mouth of a lion. He is a fearsome character. To understand this, we must do a little digging back in the Old Testament.

In Daniel 2 God sent a dream to King Nebuchadnezzar. In this dream, he saw his kingdom along with the future kingdoms in history. He dreamed of a large statue, with a head of gold, chest of silver, torso of bronze, legs of iron, and feet mixed with iron and clay.

The dream involved global kingdoms. God revealed the reigns of Babylon, the Medo-Persian kingdom, the rule of the Greeks, then the Roman Empire, and finally a revived Roman Empire.

It was nice, neat, the future all rolled up into one dream. God let Nebuchadnezzar see the future through man's eyes, glowing, shiny bright.

Then in chapter 7 of Daniel we read about these kingdoms again, only this time we see them portrayed through God's eyes, the beastly character of man's rule on the earth.

Babylon: a lion

Medo-Persians: a bear

Greeks: a leopard

Rome: a terrifying beast

Therefore, when this future ruler, the antichrist, comes to power, he will be a conglomeration of all the other world powers.

Get the picture?

Evil, wicked, beastly power personified will walk the planet and rule the nations.

When this happens, there will be only one means of escape from his deceptive power, choose Jesus.

The only wise move? Choose Him today.

The Bible tells us this evil leader will come to rule the world. Certainly, people in the past have wanted that role, but it has been difficult to imagine how that could be, and yet God said 2000 years ago it would happen.

But in recent years with all the problems the world is facing, we have heard more and more the cry for a global leader. It has begun to seem logical, even necessary, to have one person in charge. A one-world government hasn't yet been set up, but it is beginning to appear that it is just around the corner.

So, when we read about this leader who will come to power, we can now see with our own eyes the reality. We are so blessed to live at a time when our faith is also sight.

Revelation 13:3-8: "One of the heads of the beast seemed to have had a fatal wound, but the fatal wound had been healed. The whole world was filled with wonder and followed the beast. People worshiped the dragon because he had given authority to the beast, and they also worshiped the beast and asked, 'Who is like the beast? Who can wage war against it?' The beast was given a mouth to utter proud words and blasphemies and to exercise its authority for forty-two months. It opened its mouth to blaspheme God, and to slander his name and his dwelling place and those who live in heaven. It was given power to wage war against God's holy people and to conquer them. And it was given authority over every tribe, people, language and nation. All inhabitants of the earth will worship the beast—all whose names have not been written in the Lamb's book of life, the Lamb who was slain from the creation of the world."

Endowed with satanic power, the antichrist will rule. He will suffer a fatal wound, but that wound will appear to be miraculously healed, as if he has risen from the dead. This will astound the world at his power. People will be deceived and think, "How could Satan be anything but the real ruler of the world? How could this man be anything but the real messiah?"

And the response of the entire world? Worship, praise, adoration, singing offered to Satan, the beast, and the false prophet.

The Scripture is clear that everyone whose name has not been written in the Lamb's book of life will be deceived by this demonic trio.

Then the passage goes on to say: *"Whoever has ears, let them hear. If anyone is to go into captivity, into captivity they will go. If anyone is to be killed with the sword, with the sword they will be killed.' This calls for patient endurance and faithfulness on the part of God's people."* Revelation 13:9-10

The warning is clear, have ears to hear. Listen to what the Scripture says.

Pay attention.

Endure.

Remain faithful.

DAY 64

Let's take a deeper dive into understanding the third evil character who appears on the earth during these last seven years.

"Then I saw a second beast, coming out of the earth. It had two horns like a lamb, but it spoke like a dragon. It exercised all the authority of the first beast on its behalf, and made the earth and its inhabitants worship the first beast, whose fatal wound had been healed. And it performed great signs, even causing fire to come down from heaven to the earth in full view of the people. Because of the signs it was given power to perform on behalf of the first beast, it deceived the inhabitants of the earth. It ordered them to set up an image in honor of the beast who was wounded by the sword and yet lived. The second beast was given power to give breath to the image of the first beast, so that the image could speak and cause all who refused to worship the image to be killed. It also forced all people, great and small, rich and poor, free and slave, to receive a mark on their right hands or on their foreheads, so that they could not buy or sell unless they had the mark, which is the name of the beast or the number of its name." Revelation 13:11-17

This third beast arises, the cohort of Satan and the beast. He is referred to as the false prophet and his job will be to make every person on the planet fall down and worship the beast. He will have power and perform miraculous feats. However, deception, lies, intrigue, become the name of the game in these last seven years before Jesus comes to rule and reign on the earth.

And please be aware that this deception consumes like cancer. Matthew 24 identifies that in this delusion even the elect could be deceived if that were possible. The only protection from this evil is knowing and following Jesus.

As we read this it feels pretty scary, but look at how many times the phrase, "was given", is used. Over and over, we read the false prophet, and the antichrist are given their power and ability.

Throughout this book of Revelation, we need always remember, God is on the throne. He rules and reigns. He has all of it under His control and nothing will happen unless He allows it. These seven years will separate the wheat from the tares. The world will line up to get this mark. The division between the world and the believer will literally be marked with a mark.

"It also forced all people, great and small, rich and poor, free and slave, to receive a mark on their right hands or on their foreheads, so that they could not buy or sell unless they had the mark, which is the name of the beast or the number of its name. This calls for wisdom. Let the person who has insight calculate the number of the beast, for it is the number of a man. That number is 666." Revelation 13:16-18

Notice the words, "forced", and "could not buy or sell unless." Do those phrases indicate in any way, shape, or form, someone any of us would want to follow?

God is so gracious and loving. He never forces anyone to follow Him. He calls. He gently woos, and even out of His love, He sends judgment, but He doesn't demand our love and allegiance.

Here this evil trio shows their colors because at this point in the seven years of tribulation, Satan, the antichrist, and the false prophet force everyone, small or great, slave or free, rich or poor, to take an identifying number. And here in this passage we are introduced to the number that has been tossed about in books, legends, stories, movies, in Hollywood, on the big and little screen, a number we are pretty familiar with in our culture, the number 666. It crops up so much that people look at it as a fable, something akin to Jack's magic beans, or a magic lamp, not something from the pit of hell. In today's world, we dance around this evil, poke fun at it, and even embrace it. There is little fear of it.

And that's how it will be in these last years. Many will line up to gladly, willingly receive this mark. Others will be threatened under penalty of death to take this mark. If they refuse, they will be executed.

Once the mark is received, that person will be marked for eternity. The number 666 might mean they can stay alive during the tribulation, but it then guarantees them a place in the lake of fire for eternity.

There are no two ways about this, taking the number 666 is eternally fatal.

So here is the answer...DO NOT TAKE IT!

REVELATION

CHAPTER 14

DAY 65

"Then I looked, and there before me was the Lamb, standing on Mount Zion, and with him 144,000 who had his name and his Father's name written on their foreheads. And I heard a sound from heaven like the roar of rushing waters and like a loud peal of thunder. The sound I heard was like that of harpists playing their harps. And they sang a new song before the throne and before the four living creatures and the elders. No one could learn the song except the 144,000 who had been redeemed from the earth. These are those who did not defile themselves with women, for they remained virgins. They follow the Lamb wherever he goes. They were purchased from among mankind and offered as firstfruits to God and the Lamb. No lie was found in their mouths; they are blameless." Revelation 14:1-5

We have a glimpse of these men who choose to follow the Lord Jesus in these final days. Nothing, no one can deter them from their purpose. They have one single purpose in mind and that is to do what the Savior directs them to do. Their one mission is to share the love of Jesus Christ with a lost world.

They are blameless in what they do. They are identified because of Who they follow. They sing a song, unique to them because of their calling and what they face because of it.

What can be said of us?

Are we blameless?

Do people identify us because of Who we are following?

Do we refuse to compromise the message or the mission?

I understand that the calling of these 144,000 is unique. They are 12,000 from the twelve tribes of Israel listed in Revelation 11. No calling has even been like it before.

But that is also true of us. We each have a unique calling on our lives. Will we respond? Will we follow after the Lamb of God with a singleness of purpose to fulfill that calling? Will our lives create a song that is lifted up in praise to Jesus because of this calling? Will we refuse to be off mission and follow Jesus Christ?

Have you noticed throughout this book that God goes to the greatest extremes to bring people to Him, two unique witnesses who live and die for the message, signs in the earth and the heavens, 144,000 young men running around the world with the Gospel message on their lips, and now God is sending an angel with the Gospel message?

"Then I saw another angel flying in midair, and he had the eternal gospel to proclaim to those who live on the earth—to every nation, tribe, language and people. He said in a loud voice, 'Fear God and give him glory, because the hour of his judgment has come. Worship him who made the heavens, the earth, the sea and the springs of water.'" Revelation 14:6-7

Destruction, devastation, demonic activity will be the order of the day and yet, these verses assure us that the eternal Gospel is going out to every nation, tribe, language, and people. The Gospel is being offered to all who will listen.

That is the line that will be drawn in the sand. It will have nothing to do with anything except that. Saying yes or saying no to the life-changing, eternity-changing message of the Gospel will be the only choice that matters. And it will matter forever. The Gospel will go out even in the worst of times. It is so powerful that the only thing that can stop it in a life is to say no.

The enemy will not win.

DAY 66

"*A second angel followed and said, 'Fallen! Fallen is Babylon the Great,' which made all the nations drink the maddening wine of her adulteries.*" *Revelation 14:8*

This verse gives us the promise that no matter how strong the hold, no matter how far reaching the impact, no matter how powerful it looks, the enemy will not win. The enemy will fall.

Babylon was the place where mankind initially built a monument to their achievements, leaving God out of the mix. It was to prove that they were capable to build up to God, refusing to acknowledge that it would only be when God came to man that redemption was possible.

In the last days, Babylon once again becomes the rule of the day. This enemy of God looks as if it's going to win. Many in the world embrace the madness of Babylon's message and practices, so powerful that for a season it looks as if it will become the new world order. Initially it is heralded as such.

But lies will not win.

Evil will not have the victory.

The enemy will be defeated.

This message has been written in the solid rock of God's Word. It cannot be changed, altered, silenced. It is the truth and truth is true.

It isn't true because we believe it. It is true because it is truth.

Babylon will fall. Scripture proclaims it. It has been written. It will happen. No matter what our world looks like or how far-reaching evil becomes, it will not win.

The luxury of time evaporates during the tribulation. But remember, to follow the beast and identify with him will be done with an identifying mark either on the hand or the forehead. To refuse almost certainly results in death, but to accept this mark most certainly results in eternal death.

"A third angel followed them and said in a loud voice: 'If anyone worships the beast and its image and receives its mark on their forehead or on their hand, they, too, will drink the wine of God's fury, which has been poured full strength into the cup of his wrath. They will be tormented with burning sulfur in the presence of the holy angels and of the Lamb. And the smoke of their torment will rise for ever and ever. There will be no rest day or night for those who worship the beast and its image, or for anyone who receives the mark of its name.' This calls for patient endurance on the part of the people of God who keep his commands and remain faithful to Jesus." Revelation 14:9-12

A mob mentality rises by uniting to follow the beast. To reject that mindset will be seen as the ultimate offense against mankind and deserving of death, making it the most dangerous time to live that the world has ever seen. Nothing, no matter how dangerous, horrific, maddening from history equals what this time will bring.

Please hear me. This mark is not worth it.

DAY 67

"*Then I heard a voice from heaven say, 'Write this: Blessed are the dead who die in the Lord from now on.' 'Yes,' says the Spirit, 'they will rest from their labor, for their deeds will follow them.'" Revelation 14:13*

Ahh, rest. *"They will rest from their labor."*

Have you ever just longed to rest?

I have. The job before me has seemed so big that I've looked at it and wondered if I will make it to the end. But no task I have ever experienced will rival this.

This will be the most intensive time of labor that the world has ever seen. The pain, the grief, the sorrow for what is being faced and what is being witnessed are beyond our ability to understand at this moment. So challenging, so excruciating, so devastating a time, only death offers rest.

But then the rest finally comes. After breathing their last breath, these martyrs, who have not allowed anything to deter them from following Christ, enter the presence of Jesus. Everything they have experienced pales in the joy they now have,

In the presence of Jesus, their labor is over, the rest has come.

He promises the same rest to us. *"Come to me, all you who are weary and burdened, and I will give you rest." Matthew 11:28*

The text continues:

"I looked, and there before me was a white cloud, and seated on the cloud was one like a son of man with a crown of gold on his head and a sharp sickle in his hand. Then another angel came out of the temple and called in a loud voice to him who was sitting on the cloud, 'Take your sickle and reap, because the time to reap has come, for the harvest of the earth is ripe.'

So he who was seated on the cloud swung his sickle over the earth, and the earth was harvested." Revelation 14:14-16

I love the time of year when I see the farmers in the fields bringing in the corn and wheat. Baling the hay and straw signals that the work in the fields is done. When you go to the markets and see the squash, pumpkins, fall apples, it means the harvest has come in.

It will be like that at the end of time. The harvest will not, however, be fruits, grains, or vegetables. This is a harvest of souls. In the first century, the Gospel initially went out from twelve men and the world has never been the same. We have here that number increased exponentially. These 144,000 will make an untold difference. If twelve men set the world on fire, what will 144,000 do? It will be the greatest harvest of all time.

Yes, there is a great harvest coming. However, there is also a great judgment coming.

"Another angel came out of the temple in heaven, and he too had a sharp sickle. Still another angel, who had charge of the fire, came from the altar and called in a loud voice to him who had the sharp sickle, 'Take your sharp sickle and gather the clusters of grapes from the earth's vine, because its grapes are ripe.' The angel swung his sickle on the earth, gathered its grapes and threw them into the great winepress of God's wrath. They were trampled in the winepress outside the city, and blood flowed out of the press, rising as high as the horses' bridles for a distance of 1,600 stadia." Revelation 14:17-20

This will be a true blood bath. The enemies of God gathering to meet their final defeat, it will happen. It is not pleasant to think about, but our distaste at thinking about it, doesn't change it. There is coming a judgment against the enemies of God that will make blood run to the heights of the horses' bridles. This blood river flows for 1,600 stadia which is about 160 miles.

I have read different calculations as to how many deaths this means. Let's suffice it to say that thousands will die. They sacrifice their lives for a cause to conquer the world that never had a hope of success.

The enemy has done, is doing, and will do everything in his power to convince mankind that we can be like gods, knowing good and evil, and displacing the true living God.

That lie has been whispered, cheered, chanted, sung, screamed, conspired, and failed since it was spoken from the branches of a tree by an evil serpent. Any ideology, teaching, plan to change the direction of man that does not have the message of redemption, turning away from sin, and following Jesus Christ is man's attempt to usurp God. Some of those plans have taken a form of goodness and others have shown themselves evil to the core. No matter where they are on that grid, if it is not God's plan to save man, it is against Him.

It will not win.

This final battle will be a contest like no other.

But let it be said at the outset, in reality, it will be no contest.

REVELATION

CHAPTER 15

DAY 68

"*I saw in heaven another great and marvelous sign: seven angels with the seven last plagues—last, because with them God's wrath is completed.*" *Revelation 15:1*

Once again, we see sevens…seven angels with seven last plagues. In this verse, we are closing in on the end of what has been poured out on mankind. It has been incredibly challenging and terrible. The wrath has been unleashed. Day after day for multiple years it has been fury upon fury, plague upon plague.

Right now, as we are studying Revelation, let's remember that these things have not yet happened. They are on the horizon. But they will happen. Please know that our God is a loving God, but there is coming a time when His patience with a sinful world will be done, just like it was in the days of Noah.

We cannot make assumptions that actions come with no consequences. There are consequences. The Revelation has been showing us what those are. In today's passage, we see them coming to an end, but the result will be horrific. In fact, there is not a word big enough for us to understand how terrible. People will make their choices, and if they take the mark of the beast, the end will be an open door to eternal death, hell.

But let's reiterate something. Yes, there are consequences to sin, but Jesus came to take them. He paid the penalty. This is what we see in *Romans 6:23, "For the wages of sin is death, but the gift of God is eternal life in Christ Jesus our Lord."* The consequence for our sin is death, eternal death. But if we choose Christ, it's not death, it's LIFE and it's a gift.

We don't have to earn it, we cannot work to get it, and we certainly don't deserve it. But it's offered, a gift, free of charge, that pays for your sin and for mine.

If you have not yet received that gift, today would be a mighty good day to do it.

"And I saw what looked like a sea of glass glowing with fire and, standing beside the sea, those who had been victorious over the beast and its image and over the number of its name." Revelation 15:2

Again, remember that not everything in Revelation can necessarily be taken literally. In this verse, we see a sea of glass. What this is identifying is not actually known. A sea of glass could be a huge group of people in heaven, so many that to look over it, it resembles a sea. It could be symbolic for a multitude so vast and shining so brightly with the glow of God that they appear to be on fire. These perhaps are ones who have gone on before the tribulation because we see that next to them are the ones who have come through the tribulation and were victorious over the beast, its image, and its terrible mark, which is the number of its name.

The Greek word here for glass indicates a stone that is transparent. Lives that are yielded to Christ can be transparent with the glory of God glowing in them.

Could it also be a real sea made of glass? Yes, it could but the idea that this is symbolic is most probable. More and more the Revelation is being unfolded for us. We know more today than we did fifty years ago because things that seemed improbable decades ago now seem perfectly logical. For instance, years ago it might have seemed hard to fathom a numbering system that could identify every person on the planet. Keeping track of that before computers would have been impossible. Today, that is not only probable, but there are also people who are calling for it to happen soon. The closer we get to the end, the more we see how things can happen.

In these verses, we simply don't know what this is referring to, but just because we can't quite unravel the mystery, doesn't hinder it happening. Someday in heaven, for all who are believers, we will see this fiery sea of glass and the victorious ones from out of the tribulation standing right next to it. It will be quite a sight.

DAY 69

Many of us love music. Our hearts swell with powerful songs during the worship time at church. We join with joy as we sing along to the many lovely praise songs.

But perhaps music has never really been your thing. Some time ago a young man said to me, "I wish we could have church with only preaching. I don't love having the music."

That was an interesting statement and I kind of understood where he was coming from, but we need to get comfortable with it, because heaven is a place for worship and music. There is going to be singing and praise in heaven. Maybe joining in the music here is good practice for what is coming, because as believers we're going to be joining quite the music team. We are all going to become musicians with an instrument given to us by God.

Revelation 15:2-4 "They held harps given them by God and sang the song of God's servant Moses and of the Lamb: 'Great and marvelous are your deeds, Lord God Almighty. Just and true are your ways, King of the nations. Who will not fear you, Lord, and bring glory to your name? For you alone are holy. All nations will come and worship before you, for your righteous acts have been revealed.'"

This is one of the passages where people get the idea that we're going to rest on a cloud strumming harps for eternity. But that is not what this is referring to. The harps that we see in Scripture were instruments that could be played several ways. One was by a trained musician, someone who had studied and knew the notes and how each string could be used to produce a beautiful melody. Just so you know that is certainly not me.

Another way was to hang the harp in a tree and allow the wind to vibrate the strings and make music. Doesn't that sound lovely? The wind played a song on the harps. I love that.

But a third way, and maybe the way most people used it, was to merely hold the small hand-held harp up next to your ear and over your heart. You played your own music with each strum or each pluck of the string. It was your voice being added to bring glory and praise to the Lord. It was your own heart song offered quietly to the Lord.

All three ways brought music, but it may well be the heart song that we see here in this verse. We sing our song to the Lord, and it then seamlessly joins with everyone else's heart song to provide the most amazing concert that has ever been given.

As we read this passage, we are reminded that the whole book is the Revelation, the unveiling of Jesus Christ. He is the One who is worthy of all praise and glory. All accolades and tributes belong to Him. It will be our joy and privilege to join with the voices from all other believers to sing, *"Great and marvelous are your deeds, Lord God Almighty. Just and true are your ways, King of the nations. Who will not fear you, Lord, and bring glory to your name? For you alone are holy. All nations will come and worship before you, for your righteous acts have been revealed."*

It's going to be quite a choir.

DAY 70

A couple of times in my life, I've been privileged to walk through a life-sized model of the Old Testament tabernacle. In both instances, it was impressive to not only see it, but also to listen as the guide talked about the significance of each piece pointing to Christ. And it does.

As John has been viewing events, he must have been overwhelmed at the destruction and terror that he could see coming. He looked and out of the Temple that is in the heavenly realm, angels emerged. Sadly, more destruction was coming.

"After this I looked, and I saw in heaven the temple—that is, the tabernacle of the covenant law—and it was opened. Out of the temple came the seven angels with the seven plagues. They were dressed in clean, shining linen and wore golden sashes around their chests." Revelation 15:5-6

In chapter 15, John saw things in heaven. John saw things coming to the earth. He moved back and forth in this Revelation between what is seen in heaven and what is happening on the earth. In this passage he was seeing the Temple. But this is not the earthly one. This is the heavenly Temple that Moses patterned the tabernacle after. In Exodus, Moses talked with God on the mountain. For forty days God gave him the exact understanding of what the tabernacle should be. He understood the construction of each of the pieces of furniture, the altar, the bronze laver, the altar of incense, the table of showbread, the giant menorah, and the ark of the covenant. Moses knew the dimensions, the way to build each piece, so he could convey that information to its builders. He probably saw the original, so he could then explain what the model should be like.

Isaiah did see this heavenly Temple. *"In the year that King Uzziah died, I saw the Lord, high and exalted, seated on a throne; and the train of his robe filled the temple."* Isaiah 6:1

And here John also got a glimpse of the heavenly Temple. It was opened and out came seven angels with the seven last plagues.

The pain and destruction on the earth at this point have been horrible. It has been the wrath of the Lord poured out on a very sinful and obstinate world. The plagues are close to being completed, but these plagues bring with them more wrath.

"Then one of the four living creatures gave to the seven angels seven golden bowls filled with the wrath of God, who lives for ever and ever. And the temple was filled with smoke from the glory of God and from his power, and no one could enter the temple until the seven plagues of the seven angels were completed." Revelation 15:7-8

God's glory, as evidenced by the smoke, filled the Temple. No one could yet enter. But the seven angels exited and then one was given seven golden bowls. These were filled with God's wrath.

We look at some things in our world as being truly bad. Cancer is one of those. Hearing that we have heart disease is a very hard diagnosis. A car accident that causes permanent impairment can be really tough. War, and the devastation that comes with it, is terrible. Tsunamis, floods, hurricanes, tornadoes, fires that bring massive devastation are awful. And the list of truly bad things goes on.

But there is one thing that is the worst thing that can possibly happen in a person's life.

What is it?

It is an unrepentant heart.

There is absolutely nothing worse than that because it will cause a person to meet the wrath of God face-to-face. There is a place of eternal punishment. And there is no word we have in our language that can adequately describe how terrible that will be.

We are offered eternal life. Jesus gave His life, so we don't have eternal death. But many people decide to follow their own path, go their own way. Their hearts are unrepentant and become harder and harder. The people of Sodom and Gomorrah were like that. Lot ran to his sons-in-law, and they thought he was joking. They mocked truth and chose lies. They could have chosen life. Instead, they chose death.

We are offered the same choice.

If you have an unrepentant heart, the choice is death.

If you repent, the choice is Life.

Let's be honest, is it really a hard choice?

REVELATION
CHAPTER 16

DAY 71

Our dad went to the car, he thought it smelled odd but dismissed it as something in the air. The smell continued into the next day but got worse. What was in the car that was making that awful stench?

Dad was the meat cutter at the grocery, so Mom didn't have to go grocery shopping. He just brought home what we needed. That was great because Mom didn't have a car. One day he thought that he had brought everything in. But thinking you have it all doesn't necessarily mean you have it all. Dad had missed one item because it slid down under the car seat. It was a package of ground beef. It just remained in the car, heating up in the summer sun, dying a slow death. Thus, the awful smell of rotting, stinking putridness permeated our poor helpless car. When Dad found the culprit, it was too late. The stench remained for a while.

It's awful when that happens in your car.

Now think about it for the entire world.

Today we're going to talk about consequences.

During these seven years of tribulation, judgments will increase, and terrible awful things will take place. Revelation 16 outlines judgments called the seven bowls of God's wrath that will be tipped over and then poured out over all the earth. There will be no escaping these events.

"Then I heard a loud voice from the temple saying to the seven angels, 'Go, pour out the seven bowls of God's wrath on the earth.' The first angel went and poured out his bowl on the land, and ugly, festering sores broke out

on the people who had the mark of the beast and worshiped its image."
Revelation 16:1-2

God is loving. He is kind and gracious and patient, but make no mistake, there is coming a day when He will display His wrath against the injustices, the ungodliness, the evil that will be perpetrated on the earth under the reign of terror by the antichrist, Satan, and the false prophet. This unholy trio will be deceiving and enslaving the world, but God will intervene. Here, God's wrath is poured out with painful ugly sores. Everyone who has taken the beast's awful mark will become covered with oozing festering lesions. Agony and suffering will follow.

The promises the antichrist makes during this time will sound good. They will seem good. It will be something akin to what Satan spoke to Eve in the garden. The devil's words seemed logical. Adam and Eve could become like God and that felt like an incredibly wise choice. Adam and Eve got to choose, and they did. They had the freedom to pick and eat the fruit. However, they didn't get to choose the consequences. So, what happened? Instant separation from God, a realization that they were naked, pain, suffering, thorns, thistles, and death all entered the world.

None of those are results anyone in his right mind would just choose.

During the time of the tribulation there will be a choice for the world to decide. It will be a glaring choice. Choose to follow antichrist or choose to follow God. True love is always a choice and God gives the right to choose.

They just won't get to choose the consequences.

"The second angel poured out his bowl on the sea, and it turned into blood like that of a dead person, and every living thing in the sea died. The third angel poured out his bowl on the rivers and springs of water, and they became blood. Then I heard the angel in charge of the waters say: 'You are just in these judgments, O Holy One, you who are and who were; for they have shed the blood of your holy people and your prophets, and you have given them blood to drink as they deserve.' And I heard

the altar respond: 'Yes, Lord God Almighty, true and just are your judgments.'" Revelation 16:3-7

Nations shed the blood of God's holy people. In bowl judgment number two, God will turn the sea into blood. And then with the third judgment all the rivers and springs turn to blood.

Remember in the book of Exodus that one of the judgments against them was the Nile turning to blood. Their water became coagulated, rotted, stinking blood, totally undrinkable. But here in the book of Revelation it isn't just a river, or even just one country, this will be for the entire world.

This will be a time of bloodthirsty wicked people shedding innocent blood. And because they thirst for blood, God will give them blood to drink. Coagulated, stinking, rotting blood.

It sounds terrible, but God will give the world a taste of a bloodthirsty life.

But as terrible as that is, it is going to get worse. Right now, our sun behaves exactly as God designed, just as it has since God spoke it into place. The sun does its job perfectly. It lights up our world. It warms us in the cold winter days and warms us more in the heat of the summer. If we stay in it too long, we might get a sunburn and be pretty uncomfortable. If we go beyond that, there can be actual life-threatening results like heat stroke or sever sunburns. It's not the sun's fault; it's ours for being too absorbed with our activities to head indoors.

But during this fourth bowl judgment, the sun is going to go into hyper-drive. It will heat up the entire world. Scorched earth and global boiling will take on new meanings. There will be no place to hide from the burning rays.

"The fourth angel poured out his bowl on the sun, and the sun was allowed to scorch people with fire. They were seared by the intense heat and they cursed the name of God, who had control over these plagues, but they refused to repent and glorify him." Revelation 16:8-9

What I find amazing is that during this time people will fully recognize that there is a God in heaven who is pouring these consequences out onto the earth. They will know the consequences comes from His hand, but the response will not be one of repentance and asking for God's mercy. The response will be cursing and refusing to repent.

How very foolish!

DAY 72

A nd then...

"The fifth angel poured out his bowl on the throne of the beast, and its kingdom was plunged into darkness. People gnawed their tongues in agony and cursed the God of heaven because of their pains and their sores, but they refused to repent of what they had done." Revelation 16:10-11

We come to the fifth angel with the fifth of the bowl judgments. Just like in ancient Egypt, darkness descends, complete and utter darkness. And just like in Egypt with Pharaoh, the world will want it to stop. They will be gnawing their tongues in agony, but there will be no repentance, no turning to God. There will be cursing.

Why these judgments? With the first bowl, there are terrible sores. Pain and suffering follow. With the second and third, great thirst permeates the land, people will be longing for cool refreshing water. Bowl judgment number four allows the sun to bring scorching heat and fire. And then number five is horrible darkness.

It is my firm belief that everything God does, He does out of His heart of love. I believe these bowl judgments are no exception. God will be allowing the world a taste, a forerunner of an eternity apart from Him. Hell is a place of constant severe suffering and pain, never ending thirst, terrible burning judgment, and absolute darkness apart from the Creator who is light, health, peace, rest, and living water.

Why would anyone choose to stay on the path of evil leaders when the Answer to peace and rest will be right before their faces?

"The sixth angel poured out his bowl on the great river Euphrates, and its water was dried up to prepare the way for the kings from the East. Then I saw three impure spirits that looked like frogs; they came out of the mouth of the dragon, out of the mouth of the beast and out of the mouth of the false prophet. They are demonic spirits that perform signs, and they go out to the kings of the whole world, to gather them for the battle on the great day of God Almighty. 'Look, I come like a thief! Blessed is the one who stays awake and remains clothed, so as not to go naked and be shamefully exposed.' Then they gathered the kings together to the place that in Hebrew is called Armageddon." Revelation 16:12-16

Armageddon. The name has been tossed around for centuries. I have stood in this place, knowing it will be the final battle between good and evil. Satan and his followers will fully believe that they have the power to defeat the Lord. Kings will travel from the East. An army will march to the land of Israel with the absolute belief that their wicked agenda will be accomplished. How very wrong they will be.

One of the meanings for the name Armageddon is the Hill of Slaughter. How appropriate. This won't even rise to the level of a scrimmage. Jesus will defeat this enemy with a Word. When it comes to a battle between Jesus and Satan, there is no contest. The battle has already been won. The question has never been, "Who will win?" The question has always been, "Which side are we on?"

Joshua challenged the Israelites with these words. *"...then choose for yourselves this day whom you will serve..." Joshua 24:15*

The challenge is the same for us. Joshua summed up his decision with this, *"But as for me and my household, we will serve the Lord."*

I can't stress enough the importance of this decision in light of the events taking place in our world right now.

"The seventh angel poured out his bowl into the air, and out of the temple came a loud voice from the throne, saying, 'It is done!' Then there came flashes of lightning, rumblings, peals of thunder and a severe earthquake. No earthquake like it has ever occurred since mankind has

been on earth, so tremendous was the quake. The great city split into three parts, and the cities of the nations collapsed. God remembered Babylon the Great and gave her the cup filled with the wine of the fury of his wrath. Every island fled away and the mountains could not be found. From the sky huge hailstones, each weighing about a hundred pounds, fell on people. And they cursed God on account of the plague of hail, because the plague was so terrible." Revelation 16:17-21

These bowl judgments will all be terrible, but this seventh one will rock the earth. We've all heard talk about the "Big One," the earthquake that is an elimination event. And this is finally it. There have been some serious earthquakes in the world, hundreds, thousands of people have died, but this will be the one that literally changes the face of the earth. Cities will collapse. The islands and the mountains will disappear. God will be pouring His wrath against sin onto the earth. And then when the world is at its weakest point, hundred-pound hailstones will fall from the sky. No place to run, no place to hide.

At this point, there will be little time left for those who somehow survive these catastrophes. God longs for the world to repent. He waits for people to come to Him. He calls us with His love. He woos us with His grace. He judges sin and wickedness.

And right here we see the response of the world whose hearts are so far away. They curse God.

What they are unaware of is that hell will be far worse, and it is only moments away.

But eternity could be only moments away for any of us. A sudden heart attack or a stroke, a car accident, a natural disaster, our next breath is not guaranteed. We have right now, this moment, and the Bible says today is the day of salvation.

REVELATION

CHAPTER 17

DAY 73

Do you remember our challenge about the foolishness of calling psychics? You know, those who claim to know what's ahead so people can pay them money to help prepare for what's coming in the future. They claim to know and yet they didn't warn our country about 9/11. They didn't predict a global pandemic and help prepare us for COVID. One of the psychic networks went bankrupt, but they didn't see that coming.

Here's a thought: don't call a psychic, read the prophets. God's Word is always accurate and always on target with true hope. It assures us that no matter what is swirling around us we have been brought to the Kingdom for exactly this time. We have a purpose in the midst of easy times and a purpose in the midst of terrible times.

As Scripture outlines the future and we see it unfolding before our very eyes, be aware, we are here on purpose.

Revelation 17 speaks of a great prostitute. Let's define that term. A prostitute is one who provides satisfaction, but it is for gain and is without commitment. There is no true relationship. There is no life. There is no love. There is nothing outside of the transaction. This is a business deal, and it is for profit not promise.

"One of the seven angels who had the seven bowls came and said to me, 'Come, I will show you the punishment of the great prostitute, who sits by many waters. With her the kings of the earth committed adultery, and the inhabitants of the earth were intoxicated with the wine of her adulteries.'" Revelation 17:1-2

This will be the "church" of the tribulation, a conglomeration of beliefs, traditions, religious practices that are inclusive to all but will exclude the Truth. It will provide false satisfaction but have no life because the Life is not allowed in. It will embrace everything except Jesus Christ. It will be seen as the new religion of the people but will have nothing to do with the Gospel. This is a prostitute, and the world will commit adultery with her. The Word of God is ignored. Jesus Christ is abandoned. This is a feel-good substitute that embraces all, but in the end, it destroys. We are starting to get a hint of this prostituted church with Chat GPT generated sermons, church services with God's Holy Word rewritten, and AI Jesus.

There will be profit but no promise.

"Then the angel carried me away in the Spirit into a wilderness. There I saw a woman sitting on a scarlet beast that was covered with blasphemous names and had seven heads and ten horns. The woman was dressed in purple and scarlet, and was glittering with gold, precious stones and pearls. She held a golden cup in her hand, filled with abominable things and the filth of her adulteries. The name written on her forehead was a mystery:

BABYLON THE GREAT

THE MOTHER OF PROSTITUTES

AND OF THE ABOMINATIONS OF THE EARTH.

I saw that the woman was drunk with the blood of God's holy people, the blood of those who bore testimony to Jesus. When I saw her, I was greatly astonished." Revelation 17:3-6

These verses carry the description of a powerful woman. She is sitting on a beast that is covered in blasphemy. It has seven heads and ten horns. It is a complete abomination, and the exact opposite of what God offers us through Jesus Christ.

This is bondage.

This glitters with gold but offers nothing but grief.

Adultery and the filth that accompanies it swirl around her.

She offers something that the world thinks it wants, but the end is destruction.

The first account of Babylon is found in Genesis 11. Mankind thought they could build their way to God. They thought their skill and talent could produce a way to reach God.

It couldn't. It still can't. It never will.

Wealth, power, success, making a name for yourself, beauty, creating your own rules, taking what you want, clawing your way to the top, stomping your way to the top, deceiving your way to the top, may get you what you want for a short time, but the price you will pay for eternity is huge. It is beyond our ability to calculate.

That same plan will be implemented during these last days by this prostitute. It will not work.

The price that is paid by this mother of prostitutes cannot be fathomed. In the end, anyone and everyone who embraces her will follow her into eternal punishment.

It is a price that is too great to pay.

The call is to turn our lives over to Jesus.

Wealth, power, fame, glory, any earthly trappings that the world has to offer are not worth anything, but they will cost everything.

The only thing worth everything is our relationship with Jesus.

I saw a picture of a young woman arrogantly carrying a sign that read, "Going to hell and proud."

I'm grieved for her because there is coming a time when that message will echo over and over again in her heart and mind for eternity. And it will not be with pride. It will be in complete despair.

She is deceived and deceived means you simply don't know that you're deceived. In the time of the tribulation deception will be the name of the game.

The antichrist will imitate Jesus. He will claim godhood. He will mimic the Messiah and be the leader the world has created in their own minds as the perfect savior. He will be none of it, but the deception will work. The world will stand in awe and amazement.

"Then the angel said to me: Why are you astonished? I will explain to you the mystery of the woman and of the beast she rides, which has the seven heads and ten horns. The beast, which you saw, once was, now is not,

and yet will come up out of the Abyss and go to its destruction. The inhabitants of the earth whose names have not been written in the book of life from the creation of the world will be astonished when they see the beast, because it once was, now is not, and yet will come." Revelation 17:7-8

What are the details given about this woman?

She is a prostitute. She claims to worship, but she worships a false god.

She sits on many waters. Verse 15 of this chapter explains that this is the peoples, multitudes, nations, and languages of the world.

She has power over kings. They have committed adultery with her by embracing her religious teaching that is not Truth.

She is very wealthy, dressed in purple and scarlet, the color of royalty. She possesses gold and precious gems.

She holds a golden cup that is filled with abominable things and filth. This is in sharp contrast to the cup that Jesus offers to us.

Babylon represents the teaching she offers. This is counterfeit, false, destructive.

She is the mother of prostitutes and abominations. A mother should be caring, nurturing, loving. She is bent on destruction.

The seven heads are seven hills. The city of seven hills could be Rome, but this is a global religion that will embrace the false and completely reject the Truth.

She rides the beast. She is connected to the antichrist. They merge with Satan to form the unholy, ungodly alliance. But they have a limited time and then their end will come.

We are very near this deception. When we see signs that read, "Going to hell and proud", we know we are near.

DAY 74

God knows the end from the beginning. History has been outlined since before creation. The book of Daniel is one of the convincing proofs of this.

Daniel was given a vision of the future kingdoms that were to come upon the earth. God opened the days ahead to help us understand His plan.

With all of Bible prophecy, it is not a question of IF this will happen; it is only a question of WHEN it will happen.

"This calls for a mind with wisdom. The seven heads are seven hills on which the woman sits. They are also seven kings. Five have fallen, one is, the other has not yet come; but when he does come, he must remain for only a little while. The beast who once was, and now is not, is an eighth king. He belongs to the seven and is going to his destruction." Revelation 17:9-11

There have been six global kingdoms to date. They are Egypt, Assyria, Babylon, Persia, Greece, and Rome. The final kingdom will be a revival of the Roman Empire and it will literally encompass the entire world. There will be no place that is not impacted by this global government.

It will be embraced by most of the world. Coming on board and following this leader will most likely appear to be good for the planet. It may be to show that you care about your fellow man and that you are more concerned about the good of the world than you are for your own preferences. Little by little people will let go of personal rights in deference to the greater good.

It will begin as a choice. It will move to a mandate. It will then become a matter of life or death. Comply or die. It will be a commitment to a global system that rejects God and embraces the antichrist. It will include a type of identifying mark and probably even a tracking system for everyone on the planet.

This global kingdom will be touted as good for all the people but make no mistake, there will be many who profit from it. It will be proclaimed as the great equalizer, but that simply does not exist. Profit and power drive most people and this will be no different. Kings will emerge and will wield great authority. But it will be to their benefit then to present that power to the beast.

"The ten horns you saw are ten kings who have not yet received a kingdom, but who for one hour will receive authority as kings along with the beast. They have one purpose and will give their power and authority to the beast. They will wage war against the Lamb, but the Lamb will triumph over them because he is Lord of lords and King of kings—and with him will be his called, chosen and faithful followers." Revelation 17:12-14

Do you notice that in these verses nowhere are we given the name of this beast? We do know this from *Revelation 13:18,* *"This calls for wisdom. Let the person who has insight calculate the number of the beast, for it is the number of a man. That number is 666."*

We have that he is a beast, and we have his number.

I recently watched a documentary about the project in Yellowstone to release wolves back into the park to restore them to their natural habitat. One of the points that struck me was that none of the wolves was given a name. They were given numbers. The reason was that names humanize them to people. They were not being brought back to Yellowstone as pets. They were being brought back as wild animals.

The beast of Revelation is not to be humanized. He is a beast. He has been given a number. He is a destroyer. He is a wild animal. He is extremely powerful and deadly. But he is not permanent.

He thinks he will wage war against our Lord and win. He will not.

We are given the name of the leader of the pack from Revelation 9 who is referred to as the angel of the abyss. His name is Abaddon in Hebrew or Apollyon in Greek. But if we look closely at these beastly names, they are much more descriptions than names. They mean doom or destruction. Everything about the leaders in these last days shouts destruction. Their goal is to win. It will be by destroying, and their hope is to conquer, to emerge victorious.

It sounds pretty hopeless.

But, ladies and gentlemen, skip to the end of the Book.

Jesus wins.

"Then the angel said to me, 'The waters you saw, where the prostitute sits, are peoples, multitudes, nations and languages. The beast and the ten horns you saw will hate the prostitute. They will bring her to ruin and leave her naked; they will eat her flesh and burn her with fire. For God has put it into their hearts to accomplish his purpose by agreeing to hand over to the beast their royal authority, until God's words are fulfilled. The woman you saw is the great city that rules over the kings of the earth.'" Revelation 17:15-18

What begins as a combined effort becomes cannibalistic.

This is the way evil runs. It presents itself with gold and gems and glitter. It looks promising. It looks like something you want to give your life to, but soon you are entrenched in it. That is when you realize that the python has you in its grasp, sucking the life out of you, and will swallow you to destruction.

It happens to individuals. It will happen to this prostitute. The end is coming.

Please, I appeal to you, *"...if my people, who are called by my name, will humble themselves and pray and seek my face and turn from their wicked ways, then I will hear from heaven, and I will forgive their sin and will heal their land." 2 Chronicles 7:14*

The worthless promises of the evil one only end in death.

The promises of God end in forgiveness, healing, life!

REVELATION

CHAPTER 18

DAY 75

In history there are names of people we remember because of the evil they doled out. Antiochus, Nero, Caligula, Hitler, and lots of others. They did not value life, they valued power. There is one who should also make that list, Nimrod. From Revelation 17 we know that Babylon began as Babel from Genesis 11 and that is the account of Nimrod and his ungodly desire to rule from above. His name meant rebel. He ruled the land. He could be described as the first global dictator.

There is coming yet another global dictator and his residence will also be Babylon. The evil of all the others pales in comparison to this maniacal global leader. Will the residence be literal or figurative? We can't definitively say. But either way, the antichrist will be in Babylon and Babylon will be in him.

Babylon is a city that's mentioned hundreds of times in Scripture. It represents humanism, man's attempt to be his own god. Babel is noted for the tower that was designed to reach to the heavens so man could determine his own destiny.

But there is another city that's mentioned over six hundred times in Scripture. That city is Jerusalem, a city that represents man's dependence on God, the King of Kings and Lord of Lords. It represents the fact that God came down to man because we can never reach heaven on our own. We are to look to Him and allow Him to lead and guide us.

From the Scripture, we know that Jerusalem will remain. It will not be destroyed forever, no matter what comes against her.

But Babylon? *"After this I saw another angel coming down from heaven. He had great authority, and the earth was illuminated by his splendor. With a mighty voice he shouted: 'Fallen! Fallen is Babylon the Great!' She has become a dwelling for demons and a haunt for every impure spirit, a haunt for every unclean bird, a haunt for every unclean and detestable animal. For all the nations have drunk the maddening wine of her adulteries. The kings of the earth committed adultery with her, and the merchants of the earth grew rich from her excessive luxuries."* Revelation 18:1-3

It began with Babel. Later that city was referred to as Babylon. It was a city of wealth and power. We see this in the book of Daniel during the days of Nebuchadnezzar. He was the leader of Babylon six centuries before the birth of Christ. Nebuchadnezzar conquered Israel, taking captives with him. Some of those prisoners were Daniel, Shadrach, Meshach, and Abednego. The captives were in Babylon for seventy years. It was prophesied years before that this mass captivity would take place. And it happened just as God said. Then God interceded on behalf of His people and after seventy years, they were set free to return to the Holy Land.

Eventually that first Babylon met its demise. For centuries, it has been trodden underfoot.

But then we come to the final Babylon, a city, front and center during end time events, a hub for end time leaders. The demonic world will rejoice, and its residents will encamp in the wicked city. Babylon will play an integral role during the tribulation. But make no mistake, this city will fall. Babylon will not be a place for Satan and his followers to reign for long.

In Revelation, Babylon is symbolically given a personality. She is described as an adulterous woman. She is a dwelling for demons. She will establish unholy relationships with all the nations of the world and will be the epitome of evil. From Scripture, we remember that before the flood, God called Noah and his family out. We see that before the destruction of Sodom and Gomorrah, God called Lot and his family out.

We also see that here. *"Then I heard another voice from heaven say: 'Come out of her, my people,' so that you will not share in her sins, so that you will not receive any of her plagues; for her sins are piled up to heaven, and God has remembered her crimes. Give back to her as she has given; pay her back double for what she has done. Pour her a double portion from her own cup. Give her as much torment and grief as the glory and luxury she gave herself. In her heart she boasts, 'I sit enthroned as queen. I am not a widow; I will never mourn.'" Revelation 18:4-7*

Babylon will rise and become a hub of power in the last days, but the actions and sinful alliances she makes will not go unchecked. Her sins will be piled up to heaven and God will deal with her. This city will reign for a while and the attitude of her inhabitants is evident. They believe themselves to be royalty, the elite, untouchable, invincible. Babylon believes herself to be exempt from mourning.

Not so!

Plagues are plagues and an attitude of invincibility does not make people invincible.

This place will face God's judgment. Plagues are coming to Babylon and will come in double portions. Looking at the horrific plagues that have already been described in Revelation, if that's doubled, it means unbelievable destruction. Babylon will fall.

"Therefore in one day her plagues will overtake her: death, mourning and famine. She will be consumed by fire, for mighty is the Lord God who judges her. When the kings of the earth who committed adultery with her and shared her luxury see the smoke of her burning, they will weep and mourn over her. Terrified at her torment, they will stand far off and cry: 'Woe! Woe to you, great city, you mighty city of Babylon! In one hour your doom has come!'" Revelation 18:8-10

In a day, in an hour, unfathomable destruction will descend. Plagues, death, mourning, famine, fire are all part of Babylon's destiny. It is fixed. It will take place. The kings of the earth will watch the destruction and utter the two woes. Nothing can alter this. We need to always remember that what is written in God's Word is indeed firmly fixed.

We cannot twist it to fit us.

We cannot intellectually argue it away.

We cannot shut our eyes, cover our ears, and say it won't happen.

Because it will!

Babylon will rise, but then Babylon will fall, and her destruction will be so very great.

DAY 76

When I was young, I often wondered what it would be like if I were granted three wishes. Lots of cartoons and kid programming seemed to offer that. Of course, I thought wishing for a million dollars would be great. It was about the largest amount I could fathom. Growing up, my family was not dirt poor. But looking back, we lived right around the corner from dirt poor, although I didn't know it. There was always enough food. We got a few new school clothes each year. We got some things for Christmas. I thought it was a pretty good life. But back then, if I would have been asked what I'd wish for, money would have come into play. It was the American dream to be successful, to own stuff, to have a house, and a family to share it with.

Today, for many, that has grown to wanting even more stuff and perhaps less people to share it with. Luxuries and fine items have often become the goal of life. It is the idea that the person who has the most stuff when he dies, wins.

But does he?

When we consider how short our lives are here and how long eternity is, we need to realize that the here and now is a flash in the pan, a nanosecond in our real eternal lives. We need to remember that stuff is stuff. Houses will eventually decay and fall. Boats, motorcycles, cars, jet skis will rust and corrode. They are not eternal. But people are.

In Revelation the city of Babylon will meet her demise. People will grieve over her destruction.

But why?

Will they be brokenhearted because people have died?

Will they experience grief because a city is being destroyed?

No.

They will be saddened to the point of mourning because of economics. *"The merchants of the earth will weep and mourn over her because no one buys their cargoes anymore—cargoes of gold, silver, precious stones and pearls; fine linen, purple, silk and scarlet cloth; every sort of citron wood, and articles of every kind made of ivory, costly wood, bronze, iron and marble; cargoes of cinnamon and spice, of incense, myrrh and frankincense, of wine and olive oil, of fine flour and wheat; cattle and sheep; horses and carriages; and human beings sold as slaves."* Revelation 18:11-13

No one will be buying their cargoes.

Money talks…loudly. It makes demands. Sometimes it screams those demands.

It will make no difference how people get it. If they have money, they will be the decision makers, the rulers, the owners. How many times do we see people climbing ladders of economic success, leaving at the bottom of that ladder a pile of others trodden underfoot? During the tribulation period, they will buy, sell, and trade, not only stuff, but people. We often think that slavery was abolished in the 19th century. No, and as horrible as it is, it is still happening around the world today. During end times, it will be no different and most likely will escalate. Commerce will be the rule. Buying and selling anything and using the evil one's number will give the rich power over others.

Economics will be so vital, so critical, that when Babylon, a huge hub of commerce, is destroyed and the voice of financial success is silenced, the merchants will mourn.

But what about now? In recent years, we've seen the stock market take a huge hit because of something as tiny as a virus. Some people lost their jobs. Businesses closed. Some took it out on others through looting, fires, destruction. Sadly, some were so grief-stricken that they took their own lives. And economics are still challenging.

This, once again, should give us pause to reflect. Are we more concerned over an economic crisis than a spiritual one? Have our hearts been more grief-stricken over the loss of money than over the loss of people? Have we been more moved to pray for finances or for lost souls?

Those events have been a chance to check our hearts.

More events are on the horizon.

As we approach end times, unfortunately the luxuries of life will loom greater, and the value of people will wane. Until at the end, the stuff, the cargo, the fineries will be the only goal. And that will be destroyed.

Revelation 18:14-17 "They will say, 'The fruit you longed for is gone from you. All your luxury and splendor have vanished, never to be recovered.' The merchants who sold these things and gained their wealth from her will stand far off, terrified at her torment. They will weep and mourn and cry out: Woe! Woe to you, great city, dressed in fine linen, purple and scarlet, and glittering with gold, precious stones and pearls! In one hour such great wealth has been brought to ruin!'"

God's Word is fixed. The stuff that people so desperately want will be destroyed. The merchants will watch, terrified, and all of it will happen in one hour.

Today, as an adult, if I were asked what I'd wish for, it would have nothing to do with money. It wouldn't even be wishes. It would be instead what I pray for, that all my loved ones will know Christ. It would be that people will share the Gospel around the world, and it would be that people across the globe will have their lives changed for eternity by knowing the King of Kings.

But at the end doom and gloom will increase.

"Every sea captain, and all who travel by ship, the sailors, and all who earn their living from the sea, will stand far off. When they see the smoke of her burning, they will exclaim, 'Was there ever a city like this great city?' They will throw dust on their heads, and with weeping and mourning cry out: Woe! Woe to you, great city, where all who had ships on the sea became rich through her wealth! In one hour she has been brought to ruin!'"
Revelation 18:17-19

We see that mourning and grief will extend out into the sea. The people who make their money by water trade routes will also see their wealth come to ruin. They will see the destruction of the city, Babylon. They will throw dust on their heads in great mourning as the epitome of riches falls. Because money has been the goal, the loss of it will be devastating.

In Revelation 18, we have seen the destruction of cargoes, riches, luxuries, and seafaring wealth by kings, merchants, and sea captains. Three times the *woes* have been uttered. Babylon will fall and take with her the wealth of many. They will have toiled to no avail. It will all vanish.

This all brings to mind a question. What are we working for?

Now please don't read more into this than what is being said. It is certainly a blessing to have a good job and work hard to provide for our families. It's good to have a house, clothing, nutritious food, and things to enjoy. But we need to look at everything we have as a gift from the Lord and not truly ours. It is to be used to expand the Kingdom of God. What we have is merely on loan and it actually belongs to the true Owner. If God lays His hand on anything in our possession, we need to relinquish it; we should hold on to things with very open hands. We are stewards and caretakers, not owners. Our job is to do what the real Owner wants.

But the people of Babylon will not see it like that. They will give themselves over to the accumulation of great wealth. It is likened to adultery. They will lie, steal, trample to have their great love. It will make no difference who gets hurt by all the wealth gathering. The people will have had one goal…get rich at any cost. It is depravity at its worst because they will even enslave people to get it.

And God will bring consequences to it. *"Rejoice over her, you heavens! Rejoice, you people of God! Rejoice, apostles and prophets! For God has judged her with the judgment she imposed on you. Then a mighty angel picked up a boulder the size of a large millstone and threw it into the sea, and said: With such violence the great city of Babylon will be thrown down, never to be found again. The music of harpists and musicians,*

pipers and trumpeters, will never be heard in you again. No worker of any trade will ever be found in you again. The sound of a millstone will never be heard in you again. The light of a lamp will never shine in you again. The voice of bridegroom and bride will never be heard in you again. Your merchants were the world's important people. By your magic spell all the nations were led astray. In her was found the blood of prophets and of God's holy people, of all who have been slaughtered on the earth."'
Revelation 18:20-24

Here's the picture: a boulder as large and heavy as a millstone is picked up by an angel and hurled into the sea. It sinks and disappears like a rock, because it is, well, a rock. This comparison explains what will happen to the city. Babylon will disappear. Work will never take place there again, no weddings, no music, no lamps will shine. This city epitomizes the ones who have connived, swayed, cajoled the people of the land to follow the wrong path. And God has used Babylon as an example of His judgment. This city, this major hub of commerce and money-making, will end in complete destruction and it will be gone.

As we read this, let's consider what we are giving our time and energy to. Is it for our own wealth, our own pleasure?

Or is our energy going to spread the Gospel of Christ?

Each of us must answer that for ourselves.

REVELATION
CHAPTER 19

DAY 77

Hallelujah is an incredible word. It is used to express great joy and to celebrate God. But this is the first time this word is used in the book of Revelation. There has been much in this book to weep over, grieve over, see despair in, but now the moment has come to rejoice. It is a roar as hallelujah is proclaimed. Can you imagine what it will be like to hear voices from every nation, people group, land shouting that word in praise to our Lord?

"After this I heard what sounded like the roar of a great multitude in heaven shouting: 'Hallelujah! Salvation and glory and power belong to our God, for true and just are his judgments. He has condemned the great prostitute who corrupted the earth by her adulteries. He has avenged on her the blood of his servants.'" Revelation 19:1-2

This passage begins with the words, "After this..." The time has finally come for the tragedy to be over. The expiration date on this evil prostitute has arrived. She smiled her seductive smile at people only to devour their very souls, but now she is done. This false religion that seemed so attractive is over, finished, not for a moment or a day, but eternally. The condemnation has been issued.

Please hear me on this. Evil will not win. God's victory is certain. No matter what the world looks like or how much it seems like the dark side will win, it will not. It cannot. God has already declared it will end and hallelujah will be shouted.

Hallelujah means praise the Lord! It couldn't be said any better. Did I just hear an amen?

But then this hallelujah chorus will continue. Up to this time the word hallelujah has not yet been used in the New Testament. But in Revelation, it appears four times in chapter 19. This prostitute who corrupted the earth is no more. No wonder the hallelujahs are being raised.

"And again, they shouted: 'Hallelujah! The smoke from her goes up for ever and ever.' The twenty-four elders and the four living creatures fell down and worshiped God, who was seated on the throne. And they cried: 'Amen, Hallelujah!'" Revelation 19:3-4

Such praise. Such gratitude for what God has done. It is overwhelming. The response is they fall to the ground and worship the Lord.

When is the last time we were so grateful, so filled with praise that we fell to our knees? When is the last time that hallelujahs came from our lips, and we couldn't contain ourselves from praising the Lord?

What has He done for us in the last days, weeks, months? When is the last time we even breathed a thank you? What has He done?

We have breath.

We have salvation

We have an eternal home waiting for us.

He has us in His hands.

He has our lives under His control.

He has our future secured.

We can know Him, walk with Him, pray to Him.

We can pray for others and see Him at work.

Time is in His hands. It is winding down and eternity is winding up.

Ah yes, our response should definitely be worship.

Hallelujah!

DAY 78

Have you been to many weddings? I have actually been to a number of them. I think my husband has performed over a thousand. So, I have been to my share. Most of them are unique in their approach. Venue, colors, food, length of ceremony, music, traditions, casual or formal, they each carry their own signature. But most of them share one common thread. They are a celebration of love. A man and woman coming together, proclaiming a lifetime of commitment to one another. A vow is made for life together until death separates them.

Revelation 19 is setting the stage for the greatest wedding ever to take place. The music is praise from the first note. The chorus is greater than any ever assembled. It will dominate the heavens.

"Then a voice came from the throne, saying: 'Praise our God, all you his servants, you who fear him, both great and small!' Then I heard what sounded like a great multitude, like the roar of rushing waters and like loud peals of thunder, shouting: 'Hallelujah! For our Lord God Almighty reigns.'" Revelation 19:5-6

Most weddings have all eyes on the bride as she enters. She is the star.

Not this one. Yes, this wedding is for the bride, but this time all eyes will be on the Groom.

We will be so overcome with love for Him that we won't be able to take our eyes off Him. We will be so grateful to be entering His presence that we will think of nothing but Him. This is not until death do us part. This is for forever.

Our wedding day will have finally arrived.

So, what will we wear to this wedding?

When planning a wedding today that is one of the biggest questions a bride must answer. Most brides want exactly the right gown. What fabric, style, silhouette, neckline, length, even color? Most brides opt for white but what color of white? Egg shell, cream, vanilla, pure white, off-white, ivory, bone, beige... ah, yes, I could go on.

But for this event, the gown has already been decided. My guess is that it will be a white whiter than any we have ever seen. When we said yes to serving the Savior, we said yes to the dress...or the suit...or the robe...we don't really know what this outfit will be.

"Let us rejoice and be glad and give him glory! For the wedding of the Lamb has come, and his bride has made herself ready. Fine linen, bright and clean, was given her to wear.' (Fine linen stands for the righteous acts of God's holy people.)" Revelation 19:7-8

What is our attire?

Fine linen spun from the ways we have helped, shared, prayed, given, loved, made a difference. Where we have impacted the Kingdom, the stitches have been made.

The linen has come together to create our wedding attire. But the question is, what will ours be like?

Let's think back over our lives. What are the righteous acts that will make up each garment for the event? How will we be dressed for our Bridegroom?

Beautiful?

Magnificent?

Dazzling?

The righteous acts are being sewn right now. Will there be layers and layers with a train that fills the sky or will there barely be enough to cover us?

What we do determines what we wear.

Our salvation has been settled by coming to Jesus, but how we are dressed is up to us.

Take a moment to consider... what are our righteous acts? What will our wedding attire look like?

Now, think back over those weddings you've attended. Have there been some that have been absolutely wonderful occasions with just the right weather, temperature, music, laughter, and joyous tears? Have you been to any that you just can't wait to leave? Tension as some family members don't get along. Too hot in the chapel? Too much rain at the outdoor reception?

This wedding, scheduled in the heavens, will be completely perfect. We will be so excited to get to be a part of it. The word "blessed" is the one written, but we can't even begin to understand the depth of that feeling until it happens. Think of the most wonderful event of your life and that doesn't even begin to compare.

"Then the angel said to me, 'Write this: Blessed are those who are invited to the wedding supper of the Lamb!' And he added, 'These are the true words of God.' At this I fell at his feet to worship him. But he said to me, 'Don't do that! I am a fellow servant with you and with your brothers and sisters who hold to the testimony of Jesus. Worship God! For it is the Spirit of prophecy who bears testimony to Jesus.'" Revelation 19:9-10

In these verses John was once again instructed to write this down. There is a beautiful promise here. It tells us that all of us who have been invited to this wedding are blessed.

No matter what our day looks like, no matter how many problems we face, if we have accepted Jesus' invitation to be at this wedding, we have His blessing on our lives. He is walking us down the aisle, just waiting for the moment the ceremony will begin.

We are blessed. We have His Word on it.

DAY 79

We need to rejoice today because this moment described in today's verses will be like none other. We will look up and behold a white horse and the rider is the One we have called Faithful and True. He will have blazing eyes, dressed in a robe dipped in blood, and many crowns adorning His head.

"I saw heaven standing open and there before me was a white horse, whose rider is called Faithful and True. With justice he judges and wages war. His eyes are like blazing fire, and on his head are many crowns. He has a name written on him that no one knows but he himself. He is dressed in a robe dipped in blood, and his name is the Word of God. The armies of heaven were following him, riding on white horses and dressed in fine linen, white and clean. Coming out of his mouth is a sharp sword with which to strike down the nations. 'He will rule them with an iron scepter.' He treads the winepress of the fury of the wrath of God Almighty. On his robe and on his thigh he has this name written: KING OF KINGS AND LORD OF LORDS." Revelation 19:11-16

This One, our Savior, our Friend, our Redeemer, will have a new name that we don't yet know. But He will also be coming in the name we do know. That name is the Word of God. This Book we call the Bible is the name of this One who is coming. This entire Book is about Him and is a challenge on how to know Him, worship Him, serve Him.

Studying the Word of God is getting to know Jesus. We learn about Him as the Good Shepherd, the One who died on the cross and rose from the grave. We see Him as our healer, our provider, our refuge. He is our Bridegroom, the Mountain One, the Giver of Life. We could go on and on. There simply are not enough names that we can share to cover all the ways we can know Him and yet there is more to come.

He will rule. He will reign. He will come as King of Kings and Lord of Lords. We can't wait!

However, with that coming a battle is on the horizon that is unlike anything the world has ever seen. It will not be rivaled by any legion that has already marched, any weapon ever raised, any bomb ever dropped. This will be the war to end all wars. The carnage will be devastating. The clean-up crew will have to be the carrion eating birds of the air that will flock to the region for the greatest supper ever prepared for them. It will be unprecedented. It will be grievous, but we see that there is an angel standing in the sun. That angel is the one to call out to the birds of the air. The mess is being taken care of. It will mean that real peace has finally come.

"And I saw an angel standing in the sun, who cried in a loud voice to all the birds flying in midair, 'Come, gather together for the great supper of God, so that you may eat the flesh of kings, generals, and the mighty, of horses and their riders, and the flesh of all people, free and slave, great and small.'" Revelation 19:17-18.

Because this will be cleaned up, I can certainly trust Him to take care of the messes in my life. He can handle it all.

But keep in mind, there is such great arrogance in the enemies of the Lord that they cannot see that they are defeated before they even begin. This outcome has already been recorded and it is what it is. The Word of God cannot be changed.

The ammunition, strength of weaponry, number of armed men, tanks, aircraft, squadrons, command of the field or command of the skies do not matter. This battle will take place and end only one way. The Lord Jesus Christ and His followers will be victorious.

"Then I saw the beast and the kings of the earth and their armies gathered together to wage war against the rider on the horse and his army. But the beast was captured, and with it the false prophet who had performed the signs on its behalf. With these signs he had deluded those who had received

the mark of the beast and worshiped its image. The two of them were thrown alive into the fiery lake of burning sulfur. The rest were killed with the sword coming out of the mouth of the rider on the horse, and all the birds gorged themselves on their flesh." Revelation 19:19-21

The two who thought themselves to be the most powerful men of all time will be the beast and the false prophet. But they are no match for the King of Kings and Lord of Lords.

Take heart in these anxious times. He will win this battle.

The ones we face every day, that we think loom larger than life, are really just target practice.

He is bigger than it all.

No wonder this chapter shouts repeatedly, "Hallelujah."

REVELATION

CHAPTER 20

DAY 80

There are times our world has felt dark. How often have we watched a news report about the brutality of evil in our world? How many times have we heard about the atrocities of wickedness that plague the globe? When we read the book of Revelation, we come face-to-face with the great deception that Satan will use to lead the world astray. People will die under the evil. How often have we prayed for God's Kingdom to come and Satan's power to be defeated?

It's a challenge to know truth and live in a world that increasingly embraces the lies of this enemy. It almost feels at times like evil might be winning. But take heart, because we come to chapter 20 and discover how little power Satan actually has.

An angel comes holding keys in one hand and a great chain in another.

"And I saw an angel coming down out of heaven, having the key to the Abyss and holding in his hand a great chain. He seized the dragon, that ancient serpent, who is the devil, or Satan, and bound him for a thousand years. He threw him into the Abyss, and locked and sealed it over him to keep him from deceiving the nations anymore until the thousand years were ended. After that, he will be set free for a short time." Revelation 20:1-3

The moment is coming when the world's greatest enemy will be wrapped in chains, thrown into an abyss, and locked away for a thousand years. Satan's power has felt overwhelming at times, but from these verses we see that he has no real power at all. This angel can bind him with one hand tied behind his back.

Let's say it again, the enemy has no real power. He has always been under God's control. Satan can be bound in chains. He can be thrown down and then held until the exact moment when God says he can be released from those chains.

So, keep in mind, every time we see the wickedness that exists in our world, every time we feel like evil might be winning, we can remember, the devil is on a very short leash, his days are numbered, his demise is imminent. God is way, way bigger than any kind of evil.

"I saw thrones on which were seated those who had been given authority to judge. And I saw the souls of those who had been beheaded because of their testimony about Jesus and because of the word of God. They had not worshiped the beast or its image and had not received its mark on their foreheads or their hands. They came to life and reigned with Christ a thousand years. (The rest of the dead did not come to life until the thousand years were ended.) This is the first resurrection. Blessed and holy are those who share in the first resurrection. The second death has no power over them, but they will be priests of God and of Christ and will reign with him for a thousand years." Revelation 20:4-6

Out of all of the words in this passage, for me, the one that stands out at the first reading is the word beheaded. Part of the scary stuff of Revelation is this word. None of us wants to face that in our future. Not one of us wants to think about that for anyone we know and love. It's an awful brutal way to die.

So, where is the hope? If we are reading this, then we haven't yet crossed that bridge that leads from life to death. We haven't breathed our last breath. Our hearts are still beating. Death still waits. And we can push it out of our thoughts, but we can't avoid its inevitability.

But God has so graciously given us a glimpse of death for the believer, through the eyes of Stephen in Acts 7. We have already mentioned this before, but let's revisit it. Stephen was a deacon. He loved the Lord, but his faithfulness was a threat to the establishment. He gave a beautiful testimony that rocked his enemies, so they decided to retaliate with real rocks. Stoning would also not be up there as one of my chosen ways to die. I prefer a nice quiet "fall asleep here and wake up there" kind of scenario. Stoning would be brutal, painful, and not super quick. This is a terrible way to die.

But what is beyond comforting is the fact that at that moment, Jesus pulled back the veil and allowed Stephen to see right into heaven. His eyes were filled with the beauty of the Lord that the momentary reality of his circumstances paled in comparison. Jesus showed up and that is our reality too. He never leaves us. He will never forsake us. So, no matter when death comes, Jesus is there first and last and every moment in between.

And I also believe that if we are believers right now, we will be out of this world before the tribulation begins, so none of this part is in our future.

But remember, during these seven years there will be those who choose death rather than follow the antichrist. They will be beheaded because they choose faithfulness to God. They won't back down from sharing their testimony. They will stand firmly on the Word of God and absolutely refuse to take the mark of this unholy beast. They will not compromise. They will not turn back. They will not turn away. They will stand by faith in the one true living God. They will choose to live for Him and won't be stopped by the threat of laying down their lives for Him.

And their reward? Death can't hold them. They come to life and become the leadership team ruling with Jesus for the next thousand years.

How about us? What is it that threatens to stop us? Do we have that same kind of faith, that same kind of dedication that says we won't compromise, or turn back, or turn away no matter what gets thrown at us?

During the tribulation, those believers will choose to die rather than compromise. Today, most of us are not facing death for our faith, but are we choosing to live in such a way that we won't compromise, or turn back, or turn away, boldly sharing and always standing.

The time to take our stand for Him is now.

From the first few verses of Revelation 20, we see that Satan will eventually be encased in a tomb in the abyss for a thousand years. That seems like a very long time. And during that time Jesus will be reigning on the earth. The horrors of the seven years of tribulation will all be past, and the Kingdom of God will come to earth. Every person who enters this time period will be a believer. This will be the utopian society that authors have written about and that people have longed for. Paradise will exist. It will feel like the best Christmas every day of the year. Life will be lived the way it was intended to be lived. Outside temptations will be a thing of the past. Animals will dwell in harmony. People will live long lives. Health, wealth, and prosperity will be the name of the game. Peace and safety, no fear, abundant life, and Jesus will be right there. The Temple will be set up and worship will be on a scale we can't even begin to comprehend.

And the cycle of life will be evident. Children will be born to the tribulation survivors, and then their children will have children and so on. The planet will be repopulated for a thousand years. These generations will grow up never knowing the great lure of temptation that the devil throws our way.

But, a thousand years is just a thousand years, and even though it seems like a very long time, it will come to an end. And then:

"When the thousand years are over, Satan will be released from his prison and will go out to deceive the nations in the four corners of the earth-Gog and Magog-and to gather them for battle. In number they are like the sand on the seashore." Revelation 20:7-8.

Because God is love, and because real love is always a choice, God will allow Satan to be released from his chains for a short season. And Satan will go throughout the world looking like an angel of light and deceiving people with his lies. Many will succumb, just like in our world.

Following Jesus takes choosing to follow. We aren't born into it by our Christian parents. We never inherit our Christian faith. We each must receive Christ's offer of salvation.

These millennial dwellers will need to make that same choice. Sadly, for some, the demonic will look delightful and appealing, and they will join him.

It's hard for me to wrap my mind around choosing to follow the devil when Jesus will be right there. But it is hard for me to wrap my mind around why someone today would not choose to be loved and treasured and given abundant eternal life now.

DAY 81

"*They marched across the breadth of the earth and surrounded the camp of God's people, the city he loves. But fire came down from heaven and devoured them.*" *Revelation 20:9*

During these last moments of a millennial kingdom, an army of satanic followers will arise. They will receive their marching orders from Satan himself. They will follow this liar, deceiver, and thief. We do not know the lies he espouses to get people to choose to follow him at the end of this thousand-year reign of Christ, but they will sound good. Satan will promise a future that looks good.

His native language is lies. Lies in the past, lies now, and lies in this future millennial kingdom. And many will be deceived. Many will follow. They will march into a battle but will be sheep being led to the slaughter. Their demise has already been written about. Their fate has already been sealed. Fire will come down from heaven to devour them. Their lives will be over.

"*And the devil, who deceived them, was thrown into the lake of burning sulfur, where the beast and the false prophet had been thrown. They will be tormented day and night for ever and ever.*" *Revelation 20:10*

Satan made his choice eons ago. Ezekiel 28 gives us insight into this creature. He was beautiful in heaven, adorned with jewels. But he made the decision to stand against Almighty God.

In Isaiah 14 we read Satan's boast, *'I will ascend to the heavens; I will raise my throne above the stars of God; I will sit enthroned on the mount of the assembly, on the utmost heights of Mount Zaphon.*

I will ascend above the tops of the clouds; I will make myself like the Most High." Isaiah 14:13-14

His goal? To be worshiped.

His plan? To take God's place.

But his future? The lake of burning sulfur.

And that, my friends, is assured. Evil, wickedness, vileness, deception, darkness, lies and the devil himself will be cast into the lake of fire. He then joins the beast and the false prophet for an eternity of torment.

A fitting end.

Maybe you have heard it said that all roads lead to God. Maybe you've heard it taught. And you know what? It's true. All roads do lead to God. No matter what someone believes, no matter what religion, or lack there-of, that someone espouses, that road will eventually lead to God. Even if someone is a dyed-in-the-wool atheist, even if someone worships the devil and his minions, that road will take them to God.

BUT that statement, all roads lead to God, isn't finished, because while all roads do lead to God, that phrase has left off the "and". And the "and" is critically important. All roads lead to God AND the judgment.

Every person who has ever lived, everyone who is living now, everyone who will live on this planet in the future, will someday stand before God. We will all see Him. We will all kneel before Him. Every single road someone wants to travel on will eventually take them into God's presence.

"Then I saw a great white throne and him who was seated on it. The earth and the heavens fled from his presence, and there was no place for them. And I saw the dead, great and small, standing before the throne, and books were opened. Another book was opened, which is the book of life. The dead were judged according to what they had done as recorded in the books. The sea gave up the dead that were in it, and death and Hades gave up the dead that were in them, and each person was judged according to what they had done. Then death and Hades were thrown into the lake of fire.

The lake of fire is the second death. Anyone whose name was not found written in the book of life was thrown into the lake of fire." Revelation 20:11-15

And when we stand before God, the books will be opened. There will only be two choices. Our names are either in the Lamb's Book of Life or they aren't.

No debate, no question, no defense. Either...or...all roads lead to God and to judgment.

Eternity awaits.

REVELATION
CHAPTER 21

DAY 82

There have been lots of movies and TV shows that portray all manner of ways that the world will end. Nuclear war, meteors, even alien invasions are all part of the Hollywood-style theatrics. But as we've studied this amazing book of Revelation, we've seen that 2000 years ago God gave the Apostle John the vision of what actually will take place. Some of the minute details of how it all precisely plays out we can only try to discern. But any way we look at it, it will come. For millennia God has warned people that it is coming. His Word is truth, and it makes no difference if people believe it, mock it, argue about it, or theologically dispute it, it is going to happen. And it will be such devastation at the end that everything will need to be remade. We do see here that the old will pass away, there will be a new heaven and a new earth. God is going to remake and refashion His original creation to be exactly the way He wants it.

"Then I saw 'a new heaven and a new earth,' for the first heaven and the first earth had passed away, and there was no longer any sea." Revelation 21:1

About eight centuries before John saw his vision, God spoke through the prophet Isaiah, *"See, I will create new heavens and a new earth. The former things will not be remembered, nor will they come to mind." Isaiah 65:17*

When these end time events take place, there will be unbelievable devastation, but God will put it back together.

In Genesis 1 the Lord initially created it all by His Word. It will be no different at the end. He will speak and the heavens and the earth will be new.

But did you notice that the Scripture says there will be no sea? Many of us love to stand on the seashore and revel in its beauty. There is something so majestic and powerful about the waves crashing against the shore.

So why will the sea be no more?

Perhaps the book of Micah has the answer for us. *"Who is a God like you, who pardons sin and forgives the transgression of the remnant of his inheritance? You do not stay angry forever but delight to show mercy. You will again have compassion on us; you will tread our sins underfoot and hurl all our iniquities into the depths of the sea."* Micah 7:17-19

Hmm, our iniquities will be hurled into the sea.

Is that the reason that there will no longer be any sea? Our sins will be gone, buried within the depths of the sea, NEVER to be dredged up, pulled back out, or remembered again.

I once heard it said that perhaps as we stand along what used to be the seashore there will be a sign that says, "No Fishing!"

I like that. God will be remaking the earth. But there is more. A city like no one has ever seen before is on the way.

"I saw the Holy City, the new Jerusalem, coming down out of heaven from God, prepared as a bride beautifully dressed for her husband. And I heard a loud voice from the throne saying, 'Look! God's dwelling place is now among the people, and he will dwell with them. They will be his people, and God himself will be with them and be their God.'" Revelation 21:2-3

A bride beautifully dressed for her husband…isn't that wonderfully descriptive? For a woman, the day of her wedding is a time when she feels most beautiful. The dress, the adornments, the flowers all work together to make such a vison that the waiting groom tears up and catches his breath at her loveliness.

That's the imagery used here to describe how this city will be. It has been built in heaven and will come to the earth. It truly will be heaven on earth. God is going to set up a dwelling place for Himself here. And we will get to be a part of it if we know Christ as our Savior and Lord.

And there is yet more. *Isaiah 25:8: "...he will swallow up death forever. The Sovereign Lord will wipe away the tears from all faces..."*

Happiness is illusive. It does not stay. There are many things here on earth that bring us to tears. But one day that will change. Revelation reiterates what God told Isaiah *"He will wipe every tear from their eyes. There will be no more death' or mourning or crying or pain, for the old order of things has passed away." Revelation 21:4*

When my children were little and one of them was crying because of some hurt, I would often pull my child onto my lap and wipe away the tears, saying words of comfort. That is the image we have here. Our Lord will wipe away our tears. He will comfort us with the knowledge that there will no longer ever again be a time of mourning or crying or pain. That will all be behind us.

But the question arises as to what has caused our crying in the Lord's presence.

Will we be weeping over loved ones who have not accepted Christ?

Will we be brought to tears over lost opportunities?

Will we be broken over finances that could have been used to advance the Kingdom but instead were used for ourselves?

Will we weep over the state of a world that had many lost people still in it?

Will our tears be because of our own sin that put Jesus on the cross?

The answer to all of them is most likely yes.

At that moment, we may be able to see with different eyes because we have an eternal perspective. Just like it brought Jesus to tears when He looked over Jerusalem because they would not follow Him, we will weep over those who are lost.

But then Jesus will wipe every tear, the old will pass away, and we will enter into joy unspeakable.

DAY 83

A clean slate, starting over, a new beginning, a fresh start, turning over a new leaf, all are phrases for a big change in our lives. We walk away from something in our past and embrace a change, something new. Unfortunately, though, we cannot quite escape our past. It is true that when we come to Christ, He forgives our sins. We really can begin again and have a rebirth. Yet, we often remember those things from before and it hurts. Memories are not always good. It is painful to remember some past events.

But there is some great news coming. *"He who was seated on the throne said, 'I am making everything new!' Then he said, 'Write this down, for these words are trustworthy and true.' He said to me: 'It is done. I am the Alpha and the Omega, the Beginning and the End. To the thirsty I will give water without cost from the spring of the water of life.'"* Revelation 21:5-6

Everything is going to be made new.

New earth

New heavens

New us

The tears will have been wiped away. We will see everything around us with new eyes. It will be more glorious than any words can describe. *1 Corinthians 2:9 says, "However, as it is written: 'What no eye has seen, what no ear has heard, and what no human mind has conceived'— the things God has prepared for those who love him."*

God is preparing a place that we can't fathom and when He says, *"It is done"*, it will be done. It will be time to rest in the glory of the Lord's presence and freely drink from the spring of living water.

A famous poet, Robert Frost, wrote about coming to a fork in the road. He had to make a choice which road he would take. In his poem, he seemed satisfied that the one he chose, the less traveled road, was right.

It is an interesting piece of literature and in some ways a picture of life.

We each must make a choice and there are indeed two roads. *Matthew 7:13-14 says, "Enter through the narrow gate. For wide is the gate and broad is the road that leads to destruction, and many enter through it. But small is the gate and narrow the road that leads to life, and only a few find it."*

Yes, two. One is narrow, and it absolutely is less traveled. The Bible tells us that few find it. The other is wide, well-traveled, and many take that road.

But the question comes as to why.

We already know the end of each road. One leads to eternal life. The other leads to eternal death. One leads to the heavenly realm with a loving Father. The other leads to a fiery lake of burning sulfur.

Revelation 21:7-8 "Those who are victorious will inherit all this, and I will be their God and they will be my children. But the cowardly, the unbelieving, the vile, the murderers, the sexually immoral, those who practice magic arts, the idolaters and all liars—they will be consigned to the fiery lake of burning sulfur. This is the second death."

In a quick glance at these verses people might say that they don't fit into the wicked list. But let's look into a few of these a little deeper.

Cowardly

Unbelievers

Liars

Sexually immoral

Murderers

Jesus clarified these as attitudes of the heart. If we have ever looked at someone lustfully, we are adulterers. If we've been angry enough to call someone a fool, we are murderers.

Do we fall into any of these? Have we ever told a lie? Are we cowards, afraid to make a decision for Christ?

The only way to access the narrow road is to realize we are sinners in need of a Savior. So maybe today we come to a fork in the road...eternal life or eternal death.

DAY 84

For just a moment let's review. John, the beloved disciple, was sent to a prison island. It was a very meager existence. It was punishment for being a follower of Christ. According to tradition John faced persecution even before he was exiled. His life was not easy. A rocky craggy island called Patmos was where he spent some of his last days. But in the meagerness, God called John to see and write the most amazing Revelation ever known. He was privileged to experience things that are coming, things so wonderful that we hardly have words to describe them.

As we close in on the ending of his Revelation, God allowed him to see a most magnificent sight. *"One of the seven angels who had the seven bowls full of the seven last plagues came and said to me, 'Come, I will show you the bride, the wife of the Lamb.' And he carried me away in the Spirit to a mountain great and high, and showed me the Holy City, Jerusalem, coming down out of heaven from God. It shone with the glory of God, and its brilliance was like that of a very precious jewel, like a jasper, clear as crystal."* Revelation 21:9-11

The city is illuminated. It is likened to a stone, jasper. The Greek words here make us think of a beautiful gem like a diamond that catches the sun and gives off flashes of light. Only this stone city is being lit by the glory of God. It is truly amazing. The city is the New Jerusalem.

It is adorned beautifully, and it is the dwelling place for the Bride of the Lamb. Almost 2000 years ago Jesus said He was going to prepare a place. This is it. It is the home for His bride. It is like no dwelling we have ever experienced here.

It's coming, and if we are believers in Jesus, we will one day live there.

"It had a great, high wall with twelve gates, and with twelve angels at the gates. On the gates were written the names of the twelve tribes of Israel. There were three gates on the east, three on the north, three on the south and three on the west. The wall of the city had twelve foundations, and on them were the names of the twelve apostles of the Lamb." Revelation 21:12-14

Twelve gates

Twelve angels

Twelve tribes

Twelve foundations

Twelve apostles

Do we sense the theme in these couple of verses?

Our Lord is a God of order and precision. Just like the number seven in Scripture is very important, so is the number twelve. Jacob had twelve sons, which began the nation of Israel with its twelve tribes. We see in this passage representation from both the Old and New Testaments. The gates are the entrance into the city. They have the names of the twelve tribes of Israel. The foundations of the city carry the names of the twelve apostles.

As John was seeing this, he had an angel escort. The angel took him to the holy city, the New Jerusalem. John would have never seen anything that compared to this beautiful abode. But we've never seen anything that compares to it either. This is not like any structure or city layout on earth. He watches as the angel measures it before his eyes and its size alone is astounding.

"The angel who talked with me had a measuring rod of gold to measure the city, its gates and its walls. The city was laid out like a square, as long as it was wide. He measured the city with the rod and found it to be 12,000 stadia in length, and as wide and high as it is long. The angel measured the wall using human measurement, and it was 144 cubits thick." Revelation 21:15-17

Its length, width, and height are all 12,000 stadia. So how big is this? This measurement is about 1400 miles. It would be about two thirds of the size of the United States long, wide, and high.

This structure is massive. Given these measurements, there are most likely only two ways it can be built. One is a cube. The other is pyramid shape. Most Biblical scholars lean toward the cube, and I tend to agree. That would hold more people. Although either way it will be able to hold billions and every person have his or her own residence.

Then we look at the walls. They are about 200 feet thick. That alone is astounding.

As we read this, we must remember that this city is described using human language. But this comes from the heavenly realm. I'm not sure our words can come close to describing its magnificence. It's what Jesus has prepared, and He is, after all, the Master Carpenter.

Ephesians 3:16-19 "I pray that out of his glorious riches he may strengthen you with power through his Spirit in your inner being, so that Christ may dwell in your hearts through faith. And I pray that you, being rooted and established in love, may have power, together with all the Lord's holy people, to grasp how wide and long and high and deep is the love of Christ, and to know this love that surpasses knowledge—that you may be filled to the measure of all the fullness of God."

When the New Jerusalem is described in Revelation it uses three dimensions: height, width, length.

When the love of Christ is described in Ephesians, it uses four.

Hmm, now isn't that something to consider!

"The wall was made of jasper, and the city of pure gold, as pure as glass. The foundations of the city walls were decorated with every kind of precious stone. The first foundation was jasper, the second sapphire, the third agate, the fourth emerald, the fifth onyx, the sixth ruby, the seventh chrysolite, the eighth beryl, the ninth topaz, the tenth turquoise, the eleventh jacinth, and the twelfth amethyst. The twelve gates were twelve pearls, each gate made of a single pearl. The great street of the city was of gold, as pure as transparent glass." Revelation 21:18-21

Again, the number twelve.

Twelve different stones for twelve foundations, Biblical scholars have tried to link the stones that represent the twelve tribes of Israel with these foundation stones. Perhaps they do match. The challenge is that the Hebrew names of semi-precious or precious stones do not always coordinate with the Greek names. So, we cannot determine definitively that these foundations match the gems of the twelve tribes listed in the Old Testament.

Nevertheless, the foundations are interesting. Rubies, emeralds, sapphires, and nine other gems are used as building materials. They are not cut for jewelry. They do not adorn décor. They are used as building materials just like we use bricks or cement blocks. Can you imagine looking at foundations that gleam in the light because they are cut rubies, chiseled emeralds, or because the city itself is made of gold? If the outside of the city is built so beautifully, imagine what the rest of it must look like.

And then the gates are described. Each gate is made from a single pearl. Pearls come from oysters. Those are going to have to be some monster oysters to make pearls large enough for these gates to be used on a 1400-mile square structure. Everyone who asks Jesus to be their Lord and Savior can enter through those gates. And how great will it be to take a walk on streets of gold!

Genesis 1:3 "And God said, 'Let there be light,' and there was light."

Genesis is the beginning for us. Creation happened because God spoke. The very first words we hear are God commanding light into existence.

As we approach the close of the book of Revelation, we see light again, only this is from a source that we've not yet experienced. The light shines from this city. *"I did not see a temple in the city, because the Lord God Almighty and the Lamb are its temple. The city does not need the sun or the moon to shine on it, for the glory of God gives it light, and the Lamb is its lamp. The nations will walk by its light, and the kings of the earth will bring their splendor into it."* Revelation 21:22-24

God gives the city its light and there is no need for sun or moon. The Lamb is the lamp. That shouldn't be a surprise. Jesus said, *"I am the light of the world."*

There is also no need for a Temple in this city because the Lord God Almighty and the Lamb are its Temple. God is the place of worship, and we will be able to visit with the Lord every day.

Now also imagine a place where no locks, no alarm systems, no police, no sheriffs, no fire departments, no protective services will ever again be necessary. *"On no day will its gates ever be shut, for there will be no night there. The glory and honor of the nations will be brought into it. Nothing impure will ever enter it, nor will anyone who does what is shameful or deceitful, but only those whose names are written in the Lamb's book of life." Revelation 21:25-27*

This city, this amazing place, is coming. No shameful or deceitful thing will ever enter. It will be a place of complete safety. There will be no night. No one will ever hover in the darkness waiting for an opportunity to hurt or destroy. No evil will happen. It will be perfect.

Doesn't it sound like a place where you'd like to live?

So, can we? Can we each be on the list of property residents?

Yes.

There is a book, and it has the names of the residents. It's called the Lamb's Book of Life.

Each of us can have our names there.

But it doesn't happen automatically. We must each come to the place where we decide to follow Christ.

It takes a decision, and it is an individual one. I have to realize that I am a sinner and in need of a Savior. I must come to Jesus and ask Him to forgive me and be my Savior and Lord. I must decide to live for Him.

So, the question we each must ask ourselves is this: Have I?

REVELATION

CHAPTER 22

DAY 85

When I taught kindergarten, I had my entire year laid out step by step, week by week. I wanted my students to know how to read, write, recognize numbers, shapes, patterns, and the basic processes in math. We shared Bible stories in the Old and New Testament and memorized Scripture. We emphasized how to be respectful of others and when to talk and when to listen.

Our year was written down on paper so it could be used by a substitute or if need be, a new teacher coming in. It was the guide for what we wanted the kids to know. It was the beginning of their school career but set the pace for the following years.

The book of Revelation is way more than that for us as we approach the end of time. Chapter 22 gives us the end of the story but the beginning of eternity.

We approach it with great reverence.

"Then the angel showed me the river of the water of life, as clear as crystal, flowing from the throne of God and of the Lamb down the middle of the great street of the city. On each side of the river stood the tree of life, bearing twelve crops of fruit, yielding its fruit every month. And the leaves of the tree are for the healing of the nations." Revelation 22:1-2

I wish I could wrap my mind around what this exquisite place will actually be like. But my mind is not that big. I don't have the ability to comprehend something that is so gorgeous that the river is called life and it sparkles like crystals. It flows from the throne of God and of the Lamb. Do you see it?

Yes, I know, only a hint. We really can't imagine how astonishing it will be. But we can know that it will be a place we will love dwelling in for ever and ever.

I'm not sure if this is the origins for the "fruit of the month" club but it looks like a new fruit appears periodically. I have to wonder what those fruits are. Something we've tasted before? These would be the best of the best. Or are these different fruits that will bring a completely new delight?

And the leaves are unique. They have such healing properties that they bring health to nations.

Beauty, living water, the tree of life, delicious fruit, complete health...why would anyone take the risk of missing this?

The invitation to enter this magnificent place is the invitation to become Christ's follower. It is the place He has prepared for those who choose Him.

There is no better choice. There is no better time than now. There is so much to look forward to.

A curse came down on man when the first sin was committed. It has been with us ever since. It is the curse of sin and death. It means our natural bent is to go the wrong way. We serve ourselves and the result is that we are all sinners. We have never known life without sin.

But on this day, when we enter this incredible city, we will discover that the curse will be broken.

"No longer will there be any curse. The throne of God and of the Lamb will be in the city, and his servants will serve him. They will see his face, and his name will be on their foreheads." Revelation 22:3-4

I think sometimes when we see the word serve, we think drudgery, monotony, tedious, always being at someone's beck and call. Our service in God's Kingdom will not be like that. It will bring us more joy to be there serving Jesus than anything we have ever experienced or imagined. The thrill of winning a race, being crowned a beauty queen, discovering great treasure would be incredible moments, but serving our Savior will be way beyond that joy.

We will get to look into the face of the One we love the most and we will get to wear His name. Talk about a prize. His very own name will be placed on our foreheads forever. There is no name greater or more beautiful and we will get to wear it. More incredible than any jewel, more lovely than any piece of clothing, we will get to wear His name.

What a gift!

Blackouts, power shortages, electrical failure, downed power lines...we have all experienced some kind of event in our lives that meant the stove didn't work, the heat shut off, the lights went out. It's uncomfortable, inconvenient, and sometimes even dangerous. But there is coming a day when that will never be a consideration again.

"There will be no more night. They will not need the light of a lamp or the light of the sun, for the Lord God will give them light. And they will reign for ever and ever." Revelation 22:5

I have to wonder what kind of light that will be. Night will be gone, and the Lord will be the source of the light. It will be more soothing than sitting before a roaring fire. It will be more brilliant than a morning sunrise. It will bring more rest than the golds, oranges, reds, pinks of the sun going down. The Northern Lights will be no comparison. Candlelight, oil lamps, even the giant menorahs that once stood in the Temple court will be no match. This light will come directly from God.

We have hints today of the beauty that comes from light. But even the most breathtaking is only a hint. That day...nothing will compare.

DAY 86

"*The angel said to me, 'These words are trustworthy and true. The Lord, the God who inspires the prophets, sent his angel to show his servants the things that must soon take place.'*" Revelation 22:6

John was one of the original twelve disciples. He walked with Jesus. He leaned on Him during the Last Supper. He was the one to whom Jesus entrusted the care of His mother. And yet, hard things accompanied John's life. Remember, John was sentenced to exile on a rock filled island called Patmos. He was there because he had the audacity to share His testimony of Jesus and speak the Word of God. The world at that time thought a just punishment for those high crimes was exile, living alone, a stripped-down version of a life.

But also remember the beauty God surrounded John with and engulfed him in. An angel came and showed him this glorious vision of the future. Things that John couldn't even begin to imagine were opened for his preview. God also lifted the veil on the heavenly Kingdom. He saw a new earth. He saw a new heaven. How often during his lonely days did he look back and remember the magnificence of the vision? How much of his time was filled with reliving the majesty and glory that can only accompany God's revelation?

Here the angel speaks and confirms that everything John has seen, heard, experienced, and lived through is true. It is trustworthy. He can stand on it. He can stake his life on it. And God sent it, not just for John, but for us, for all of us who call ourselves servants of God. This amazing vision of the future, whether very near or a little farther in the future is here for us.

So, when we feel stressed or overwhelmed by what life throws at us, we can also glory in the vision that God has shared with us.

Here in these pages, we can live and breathe the future and see and hear the glory that awaits us. Dear friends it all is waiting for us. It is our future if we know Him. Why would anyone want to miss this glorious life?

And we have this promise,

"Look, I am coming soon! Blessed is the one who keeps the words of the prophecy written in this scroll." Revelation 22:7

And that is the blessed hope. He is coming soon. When life gets hard, remember, He is coming soon. When circumstances overwhelm, He is coming soon. When loved ones die, and the grief seems unbearable, He is coming soon.

In the beginning of this study, we mentioned that the book of Revelation opens with a three-fold blessing. It is the only book in the Bible that makes such a claim. We will be blessed if we read it. We will be blessed if we hear it. We will be blessed if we take the words to heart, in other words, do what is says. Read, hear, and obey. And here at the end we see the same promise. *"Blessed is the one who keeps the words of the prophecy written in this scroll."*

So, a one-time read through isn't enough. This book, along with every other word God has written, needs to become part of our DNA. We need to read it, listen to it, study it, stand on it, feast on it, chew on it, meditate on it, discuss it, wrestle with it, trust it, breathe it, obey it, live it and give our lives to it.

This promise is a big one. We will be blessed if we keep the words of this prophecy.

When the pandemic started and fear swirled around our world and the rug in our lives kept getting pulled in all directions, I often put this book on and listened to the words. And every time felt wrapped up in the loving arms of the Lord. There is peace here for the believer. There is joy in His promises.

There is rest from the chaos of the world because He ushers us into His sweet calming presence.

And over and over we are reminded that our God was and is and always will be on the throne.

This book is powerful, overwhelming, John felt the power.

"I, John, am the one who heard and saw these things. And when I had heard and seen them, I fell down to worship at the feet of the angel who had been showing them to me. But he said to me, 'Don't do that! I am a fellow servant with you and with your fellow prophets and with all who keep the words of this scroll. Worship God!'" Revelation 22:8-9

John was overcome. He was astounded by the future. He stood amazed at the revelation and the worship was right there, oozing out of him, but he chose the wrong one to worship. He fell down before the angel who had brought him this magnificent Revelation. He began to worship an angel. The angel had to set him straight. He let John know in no uncertain terms that angels are not to be worshiped. That honor is only for the Lord. The admonition is direct and straight forward.

"Worship God!"

Angels know the truth, only God deserves our worship.

Anyone or anything that comes before the Lord and demands our worship is a false god, a substitute for the real. We have to ask ourselves the question, is there anyone or anything more important to us than the Lord. If so, the angel is speaking to us today.

"Worship God!"

DAY 87

"*Then he told me, 'Do not seal up the words of the prophecy of this scroll, because the time is near.'*" *Revelation 22:10*

Back in the Old Testament, when God sent an angel to Daniel and gave him a revelation of the future, Daniel was told to seal up the book for a future time.

Daniel 12:4 "But you, Daniel, roll up and seal the words of the scroll until the time of the end. Many will go here and there to increase knowledge."

But here, John is told not to seal this book. The reason? We are given the answer. *"Because the time is near."* That was 2000 years ago. So, how much nearer are we now?

With every passing day it is closer. Pandemics, riots, lootings, killings, with each new event on the horizon, it feels closer. The way our world is going I have to wonder if we aren't very, very close to breathing celestial air.

And now we do have the privilege of unpacking the book of Daniel and unsealing those verses. We have the joy of jumping in and studying this wonderful book of Revelation. We have the honor of seeing with our own eyes events happening in our world that help us understand the prophecy even more. We are truly living in an amazing time because God is giving us eyes to see.

The time is near!

And all of that is encouraging and hopeful, but the very next verse in Revelation is a frightening one.

"Let the one who does wrong continue to do wrong; let the vile person continue to be vile; let the one who does right continue to do right; and let the holy person continue to be holy." Revelation 22:11

There is a dividing line. There is wrong and there is right. We live in a world that thinks we can mix the two. We don't have that right. We can't rename something good that God has already condemned. God's Word is the plumb line. There is vileness and there is holiness. What God says is vile is vile. What God deems as holy is holy. We humans don't get to change what God says. And what this verse is telling us is that there is coming a time when the season for choosing which side of this fence we want to be on will be over. The person who has chosen the broad path, the one filled with self, and pride, and evil, and vile will be beyond the reach of what is right and holy and good. The path will be set, the destiny unchangeable.

And we are without excuse. We have the Book. We can read or listen to the Bible any time of the day or night. It's available on our TV's, our computers. We can read it on our phones. The truth is always at our fingertips.

And any excuses won't hold water, and every person will actually recognize that they are without excuse.

The Bible says that today is the day of salvation for a reason. How dreadfully sad for the person who thinks they can wait one more day to choose the right, only to discover that they have waited one day too long.

Hell is way too long to regret that decision.

DAY 88

When I say the word, "soon" what comes to mind?

A few minutes? A few days? A few months?

We say things like, "I'll pick you up soon." Or, "I'll be retiring soon." Or, "Soon the rain will come."

The word soon is a relative term. It does not have a definite time stamp. This is not quite like "I'll pick you up at 12:00 PM. Or, "I'll be retiring at the end of this year." Or, "Starting at three o'clock this afternoon, there is a 100% chance of rain."

Yes, the word soon is a relative term. But Jesus used it in the next passage. *"Look, I am coming soon! My reward is with me, and I will give to each person according to what they have done. I am the Alpha and the Omega, the First and the Last, the Beginning and the End." Revelation 22:12-13*

He told John He was coming soon. John penned this close to two thousand years ago. So, if it was soon for John, it is certainly sooner for us.

As we've looked at John's Revelation of Christ, we have seen both glorious and frightening events that are on the horizon.

That should cause us to pause and reflect. Do we want to face the tribulation? Do we want our children, grandchildren, friends, loved ones to face the tribulation? The answer to that is no!

As we've seen the plagues, the devastations that are coming for those who remain after the rapture, it should be that we absolutely don't want anyone we know and love to be here for it.

If we knew that Jesus was coming for the church tomorrow, how would we spend today? Would we tell loved ones about Jesus? Would we share with co-workers and maybe even casual acquaintances?

Jesus is coming soon, and He is bringing His reward with Him.

If we are reading this today, it means we still have time. But the events of Revelation are close at hand.

On God's time clock are we at 11:59:59?

We don't know, but what we do know is that it is soon.

The next two verses in this chapter are side by side, but they are as different from each other as day is from night. Verse 14 represents those who walk in light, while verse 15 is about those who have chosen the darkness.

"Blessed are those who wash their robes, that they may have the right to the tree of life and may go through the gates into the city" Revelation 22:14

"Outside are the dogs, those who practice magic arts, the sexually immoral, the murderers, the idolaters and everyone who loves and practices falsehood." Revelation 22:15

It is heartbreaking that anyone would be on the outside of God's Kingdom. Jesus came to bring the free gift of salvation to any who will receive it. Yet there are those who reject this gift.

The first group have washed their robes. These robes stand for their lives, which have been washed clean by the blood of the Lamb. There is no filth, no sin, no dirt of any kind because Jesus took it all on Himself at the cross. This group has come to Him and asked for forgiveness. They are now robed in the righteousness of Christ. This group is blessed beyond measure. The tree of life will be accessible to all who dwell in God's Kingdom. Those who have accepted Christ will live forever with Him.

But outside there will be weeping, wailing. Their choices will have been made and the decision time will be over. They will never be able to enter the beautiful city of God. They will never experience the great love of the Lord. They will live in darkness, fear, pain, agony.

Eternity will go on and on and on.

We really have no frame of reference for that. Humans understand beginnings and ends.

But eternity has no end.

Two different scenes as different as day and night, light and darkness.

If you haven't already done so, please, choose Light.

DAY 89

"*I, Jesus, have sent my angel to give you this testimony for the churches. I am the Root and the Offspring of David, and the bright Morning Star.*" *Revelation 22:16*

John was maybe in his nineties when he received this amazing gift. In the midst of being a prisoner in a desolate place, God revealed events to him that are astounding. The Revelation was given to a single person, John. Then he wrote it down. But also, here in verse 16, we see something interesting. Jesus is speaking to John and yet when He uses the word "you" he uses the plural form.

In English, it doesn't matter if we are speaking to one person or a group, we use the word you, and the context helps us understand if it is singular or plural. Here the Greek actually delineates which is used. And this time the word you is plural.

Jesus was giving this Revelation to John, but also for all of us. Way back, almost two thousand years ago, you and I were included. Jesus was giving this testimony for all, churches, individuals, any who would read and accept it.

Jesus, the Root and the Offspring of David, the bright Morning Star, Savior, Lord, King of Kings, is speaking to you. He is speaking to me.

Sometimes in the night I wake up extremely thirsty. Most nights I fill up a very large glass of ice water to sit next to my bed so it is right there, and I can get a drink. It is a terrible thing to feel parched and not be able to have my thirst quenched. Ice cold water is truly a delightful thing.

The problem is we get thirsty again and again.

Our souls are thirsty too. We have within us a void that can only be filled by Jesus. We thirst for water, but it is not H_2O. It is Living Water.

In John 4, Jesus made a trip through Samaria. He sat down by a well, and a woman came to draw some water. Jesus already knew this interaction was going to take place. It is why He had to go that way. He knew that she needed a divine appointment. During the conversation, He told her something that was completely astounding to her. *"If you knew the gift of God and who it is that asks you for a drink, you would have asked him and he would have given you living water."*

He offered her living water.

Here's something that should be completely astounding to us. He offers us living water too.

"The Spirit and the bride say, 'Come!' And let the one who hears say, 'Come!' Let the one who is thirsty come; and let the one who wishes take the free gift of the water of life." Revelation 22:17

We are being summoned.

We have a divine appointment.

Right now, this very moment, God is calling, "Come!"

If you have never experienced the thirst-quenching living water of the Lord, then, "Come!" Take the free gift of the water of life.

Just like for the woman at the well, it is an eternity-changing drink.

DAY 90

Revelation: A Treasure Hunt has been a joy for us to write and share. To all of you, our readers, we wish to say thank you for joining us on this adventure.

"I make known the end from the beginning, from ancient times, what is still to come. I say, 'My purpose will stand, and I will do all that I please.'" Isaiah 46:10

God, through His Word, has revealed His Truth. He wants His people informed.

Remember back to Revelation chapter 5. We saw that the Lamb was found worthy to open the scroll. Of course, we know that the Lamb is Jesus. He revealed to John events that were in the future.

That future is closer for us today.

Walking through Revelation means studying the contents of the scroll as it has been opened for us. It has unfurled plagues and devastation that we cannot comprehend. It has also unveiled blessings and promises for us who are believers. The words were true for John; they are true today and will happen exactly as God has ordained. In Matthew 24 the disciples asked Jesus about end time events. This passage is referred to as the Olivet Discourse. Jesus shared lots of signs that would come. Then He made a statement in verse 28, *"Wherever there is a carcass, there the vultures will gather."*

I was pulling out of my driveway and looked up. I saw a very large bird kind of swooping down and I caught a glimpse of its head. Immediately, I knew it was a vulture.

As I stared, I saw a whole bunch of them swirling. Suddenly I knew that somewhere in my neighborhood some animal had met its demise and that its carcass was somewhere close. The vultures were proof positive. Jesus told his disciples that when the signs would come together and congregate like birds swirling in the sky, they would know that the end was near.

Jesus also told them that the signs would come as labor pains. At the end of labor, right before the birth, those pains come fast and furious. Today the signs are swirling and coming faster and faster.

As we have read Revelation, we've seen that happening

Over the years, some have tried to negate the message of this book. They have scoffed at it, tried to water it down, taken parts of it away, or added to what it says. For those who have attempted to change it, there is a warning. *"I warn everyone who hears the words of the prophecy of this scroll: If anyone adds anything to them, God will add to that person the plagues described in this scroll. And if anyone takes words away from this scroll of prophecy, God will take away from that person any share in the tree of life and in the Holy City, which are described in this scroll." Revelation 22:18-19*

That is a very stern warning with a very severe punishment attached to it. God knew what He wanted us to know and that's what He gave John. God's Word is perfect exactly the way it was written.

Revelation isn't a book to be read once and then set aside. New blessings come each time we open its pages. It is beautiful. It is frightening, but the beauty and fear can collide to bring about the awe and reverence it deserves.

And as we end, we come to one final passage. It is Jesus' declaration of His soon coming and John's lovely affirmation of his hope.

"He who testifies to these things says, 'Yes, I am coming soon.' Amen. Come, Lord Jesus. The grace of the Lord Jesus be with God's people. Amen." Revelation 22:20-21

It is our hope also!
Come, Lord Jesus.
Amen.

ABOUT THE AUTHORS

The Kandel Sisters are Kris Kandel Schwambach, Karen Kandel Kizlin, Kathie Kandel Poe and Linda Kandel Mason.

As mothers, grandmothers and Bible teachers, these sisters write to reveal a sense of wonder, discovery and love for God and the Bible.

OTHER BOOKS:

DEVOTIONALS
Take A Deep Breath...It's Christmas
Catch Your Breath...It's A New Beginning
The Resurrection...It's Breathtaking
Get On Your Knee Replacements And Pray (Hachette)

CHILDREN'S FICTION
The Adventure On Rodentia Drive

ADULT FICTION
Scarred

Website: thekandelsisters.com
Facebook: @thekandelsisters

Made in the USA
Middletown, DE
02 September 2024